Heavy Metaling....

The Artwork of David Kettler

Heavy Metaling....the artwork of David Kettler

Dedication Page

This compilation is dedicated to my late Father in law, Lloyd Wirtjes. I miss him and think about him many times through each week. Many of the tools that I use in my artwork are from his shop collection and every time I grab that massive hand-grinder that seems to weigh about a ton, I think about Lloyd! His career was metal plate sales, grinding, flame cutting and fabrication. I'm pretty sure that my artistic endeavors in metal began after he had passed. I really wish he could see my work.

Of course I want to thank my wonderful long-suffering wife. I want to thank my three wonderful boys, my mom, my mother-in-law, my brothers, sister and many supportive friends. Thank you to Yuri Spilny who is a constant support and encouragement as well as a very tech-savy eighty year old! Thank you most of all...to my Creator. Without whom, nothing would be possible. I like to think that everything we do that is Loving or Beautiful is a reflection of the Master Creator that resides within us.

How did this all start? It seems like I was about eight or nine when my dad taught me to weld on our little buzz box arc welder at home in Anaheim. I was in welding classes all through junior high school and in high school as well. I never pursued welding as a career but I have always enjoyed it and have found myself constructing many things over the years that pertained to the wholesale business that I currently manage.

About two years ago, we were in South Lake Tahoe to meet my oldest son who was doing some training there. Myself, my wife and our middle son wandered into an art gallery located near the gondola just to pass the time and I spotted some wood and metal pieces that really sparked my attention! I thought..."I could build that!" Sure enough, when we got home, I replicated to the best of my ability a wall piece that I called, "Prairie Wind."

Having met the President of our local art association, I asked her if she would be interested displaying it in the gallery. Iva told me to do two more pieces and she would propose them to the board. With three different pieces, they would get a better idea of my artistic style. I proceeded to build "Art Explosion" and "Golden State" which was the state of California in plate steel mounted in an old plow disc. The board liked my work and invited me to display in one of their windows. My work has been there ever since and I am very grateful to Bakersfield Art Association for their wonderful support, encouragement and friendship.

Since that time, I have been expanding my part time hobby to include other places that are displaying my work. I kind of like to think of my art split down the middle. Some of my art pieces are strictly for fun and I don't really care if I sell them or not. The other part is making really cool recognition pieces that are very unique and not the run-of-the-mill trophies or plaques. I really enjoy finding unique pieces of scrap metal and making something out of it. Sometimes my friend Don will call me and say..."hey I found a really neat old metal piece off of an old tractor, maybe you can make something out of it!" I hope you enjoy perusing my work as much as I enjoy making it!

Create

A piece of metal on its own
sitting in the garage at home
Doing nothing for itself
laying useless on a shelf

In my mind a plan concocts
using metal wood and rocks
By themselves they useless be
but together you will see

Wheels turning can create
something of their empty state
Maybe useful or sublime…
or beautiful in their own time

To be remembered more than naught
something new of which was wrought
The metal had to feel some pain
sawing goes against the grain

Breaking of the rocks must be
for convergence of the three
So together they will stay
in a new and different way

Transformed and changed
by hand of fate
All brought about…
when I create

David Kettler, 10/05/10

Table of Contents

Art Pieces

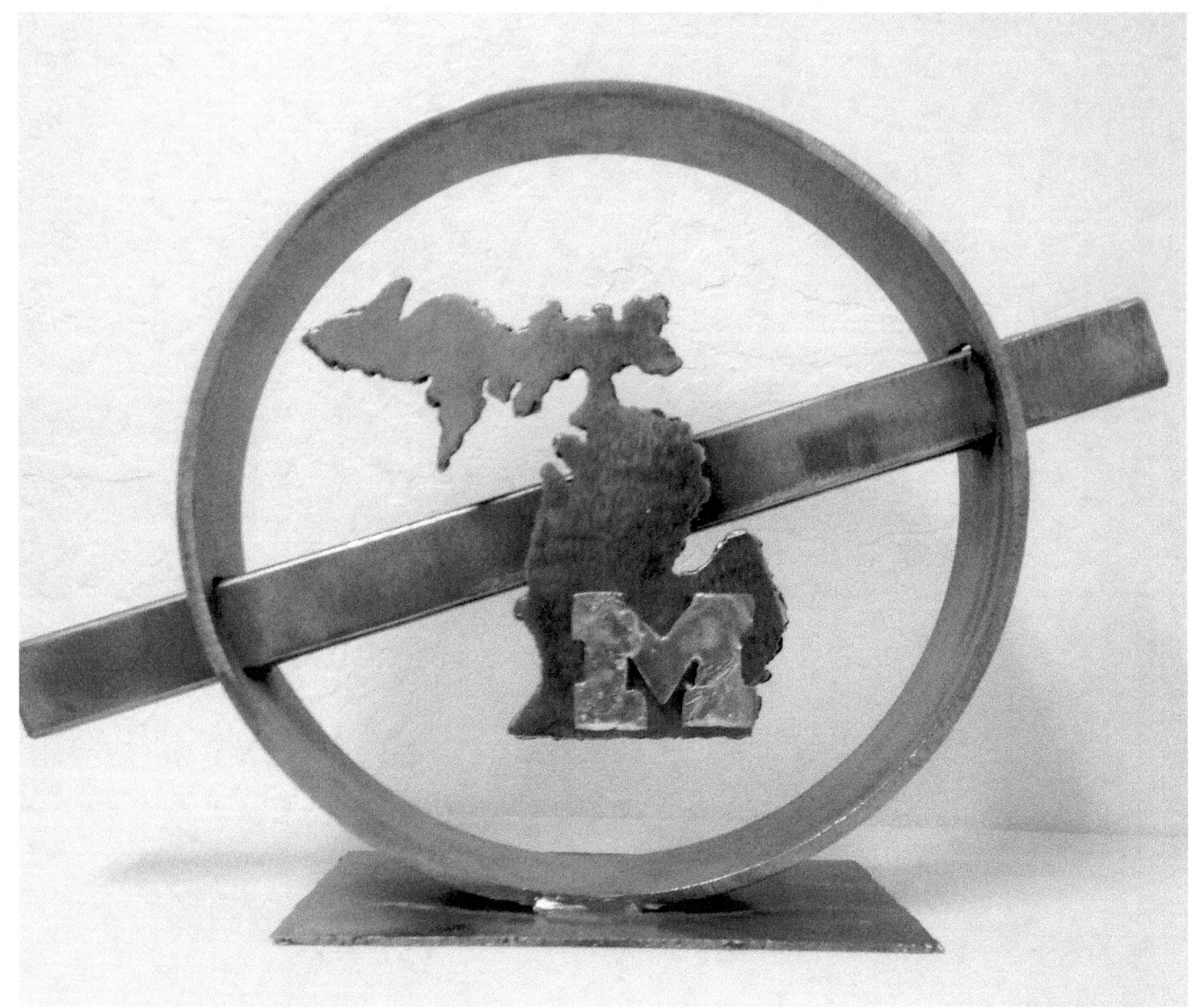

This is Michigan and I did it for Sue who also purchased "Nature & Nurture II." It is the state of Michigan cut out of plate metal and then the bronzed "M" down south approx. where Ann Arbor is located. She is an alumna of The University of Michigan.

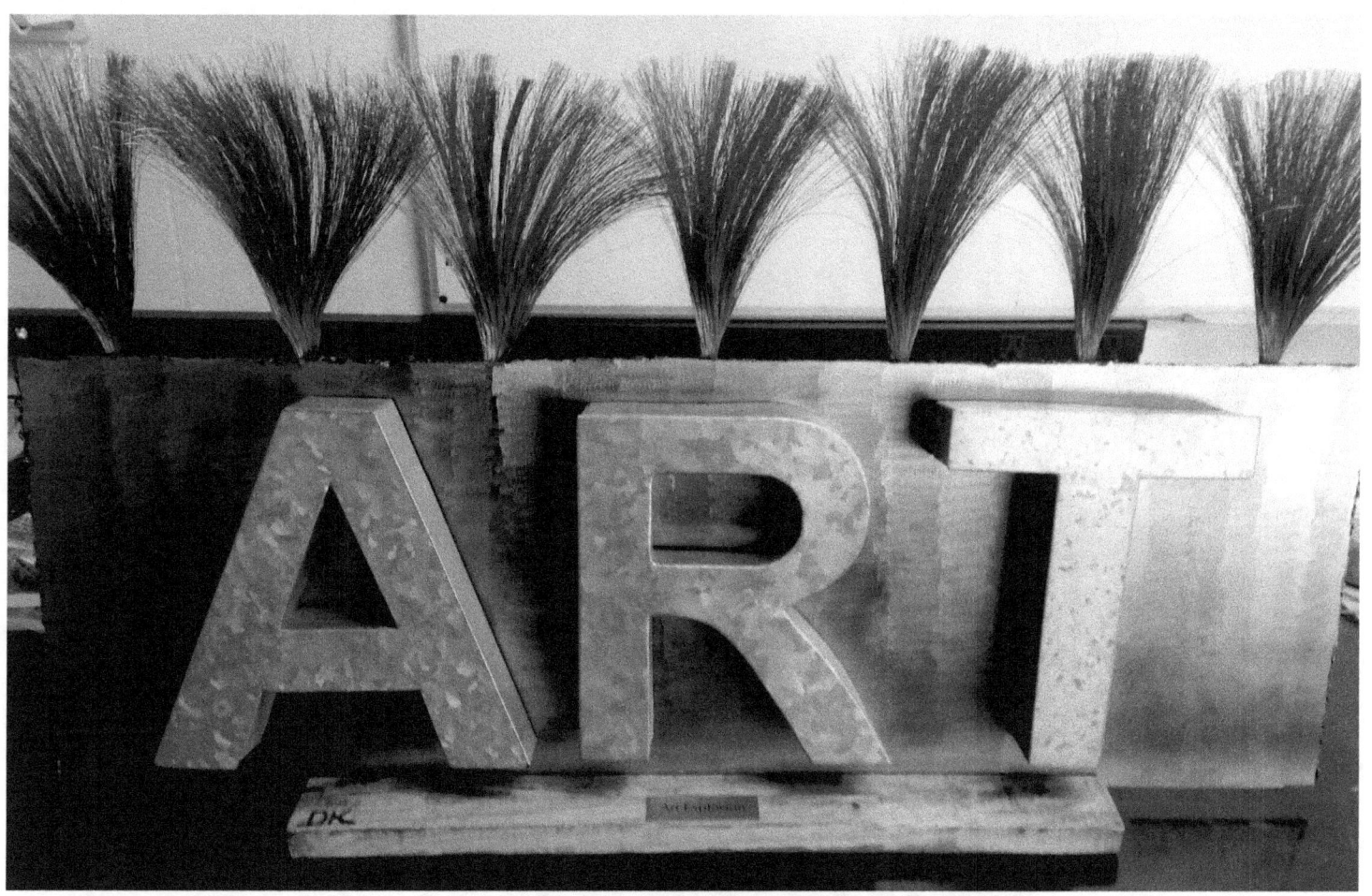

This was the second art piece I made as a sample of my work for The Bakersfield Art Association. I used a wood base and plate steel upon which I mounted the pre-made metal letters. The "explosions" are actually battery cable that I secured on the back of the metal plate and then wire brushed them.

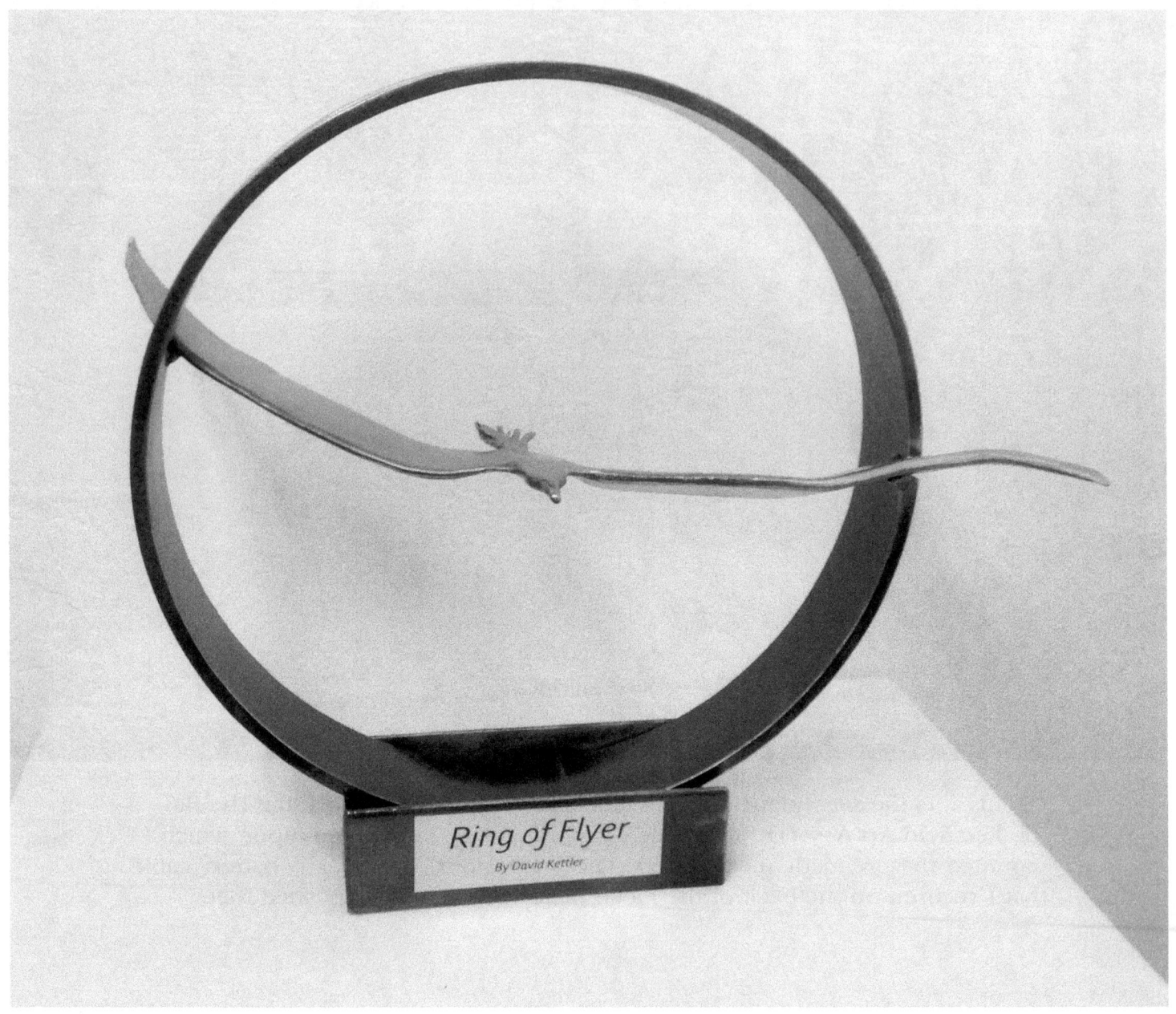

Ring of Flyer

By David Kettler

This piece was a kick to create! The ring came about because my friend Don called me and said that he had something I might be interested in. Don is a heavy diesel mechanic in Bakersfield and he often comes up with interesting pieces from weird tractors or machines. We never could decide what the ring was actually from. Our mutual friend thinks it might have come off of a large irrigation pump system. Anyway, I started thinking about how I was going to use it and I envisioned some kind of bird flying in it. The seagull started out as a piece of grader blade that had been put into the scrap metal bin. I rough-cut the bird out with a cutting torch and just started forming it, bending it and grinding it into a seagull in flight. The base was from a back-up battery system that I demoed out about eight years ago. I needed something heavy and sturdy to hold the weighty piece and it did the trick perfect. The name "Ring of Flyer" is a take-off of the Johnny Cash song, "Ring of Fire." I just thought it sounded cool.

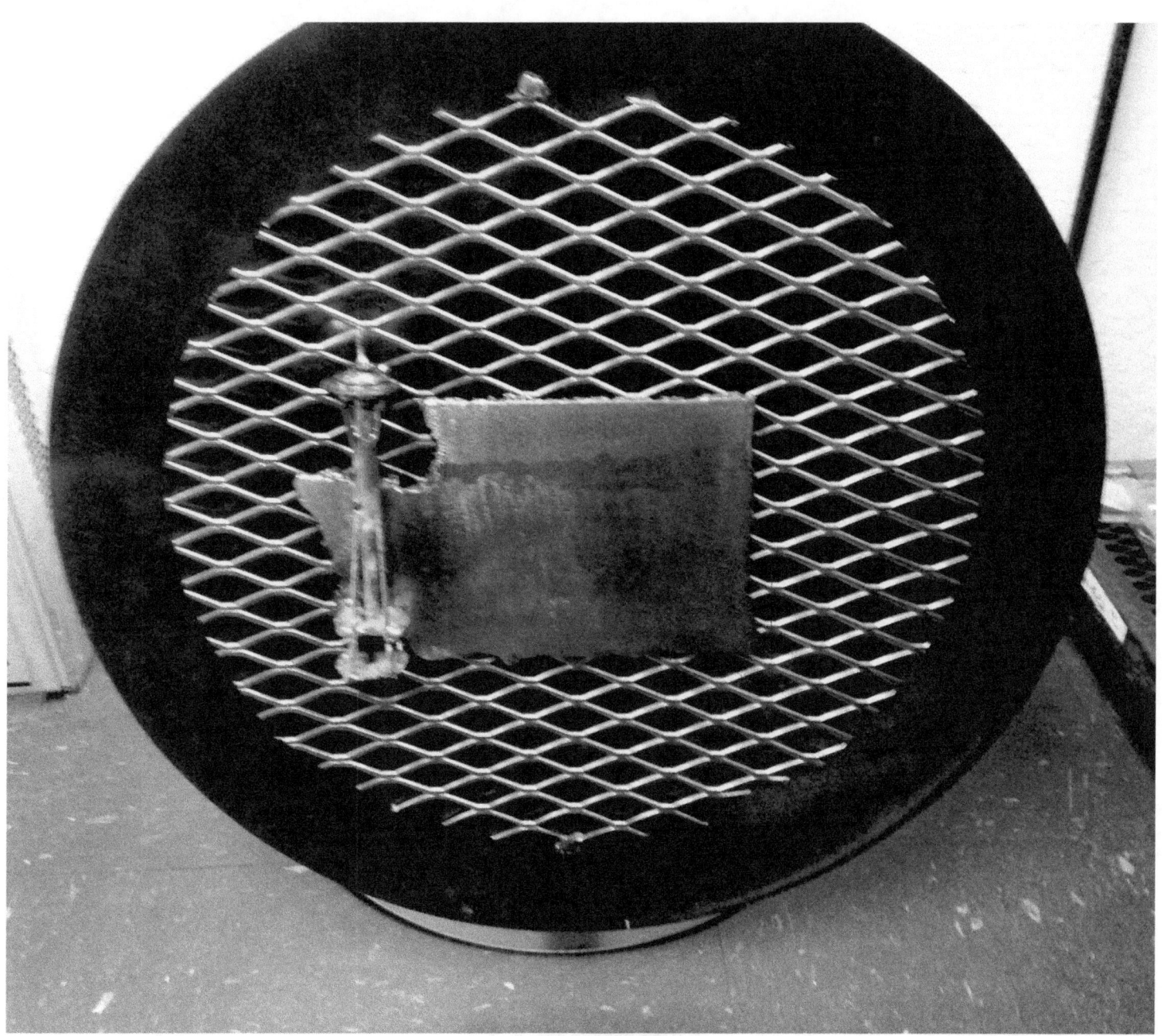

This was the piece I created for my dear friend Eugene. It is the state of Washington cut out of plate steel and laid on the wire mesh which then in turn is attached to an old plow disc. For the Space Needle, I just looked at pictures of the real thing and then started trying to copy that using whatever I could find lying around! Some scrap square stock, old metal coat hangers, washers, nuts and then I bronzed the whole thing.

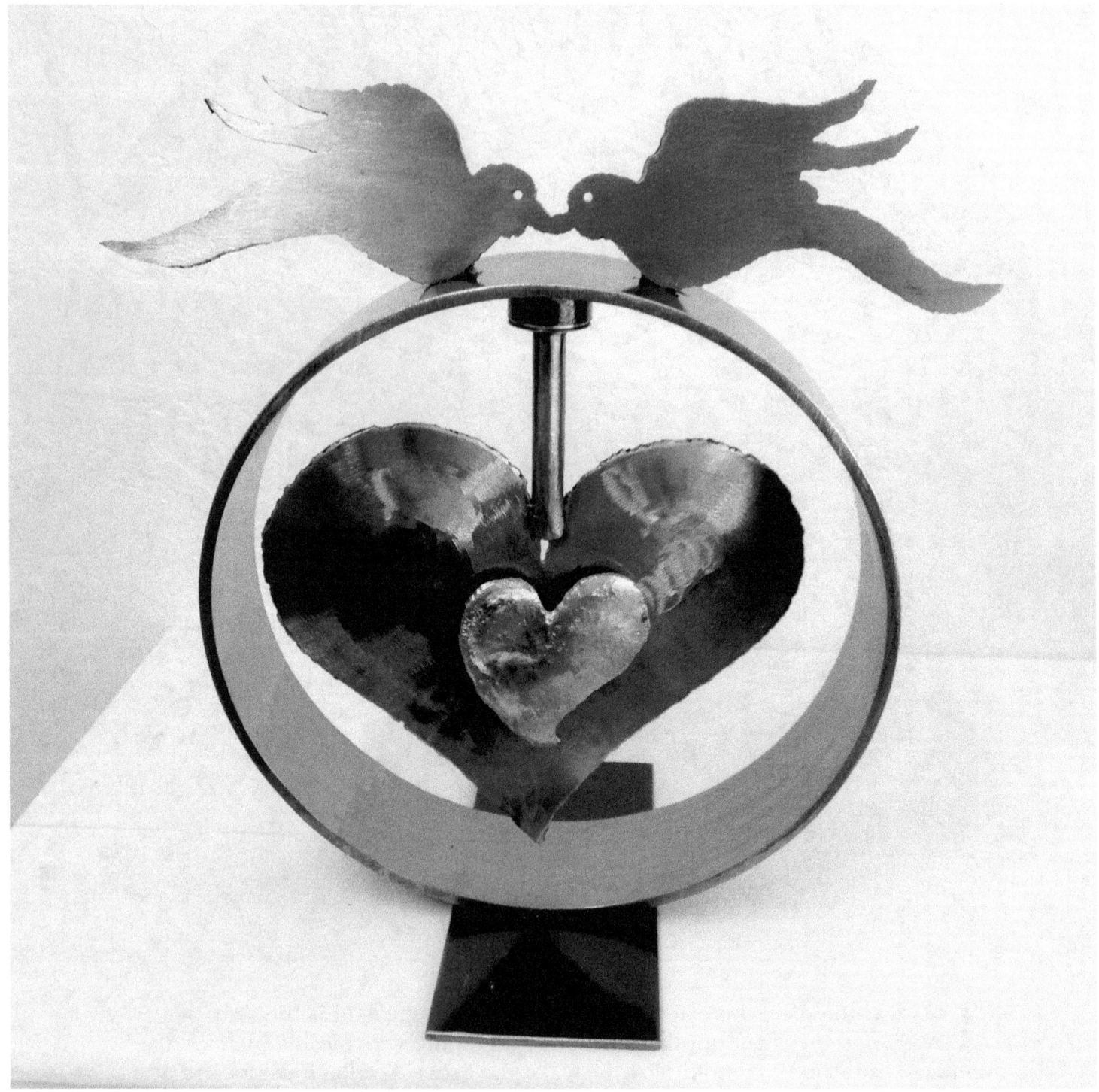

This was inspired from an artist call given out by the "Porch" store in Carpentaria California. The theme was "The nature of Love" and this was my submission. It was a real hit in the show and it sold immediately! I have since sold "Nature & Nurture II" to my friend Sue and I am working on "Nature & Nurture III which will go on sale at the Porch Store later next month. I hand cut the birds and the hearts out of plate steel with a cutting torch, and then mounted the heart on an extra wheel bearing that I had laying around. There are smaller bronzed hearts on both sides which are visible when it's turning around. I have made small alterations in each of the following N&N pieces.

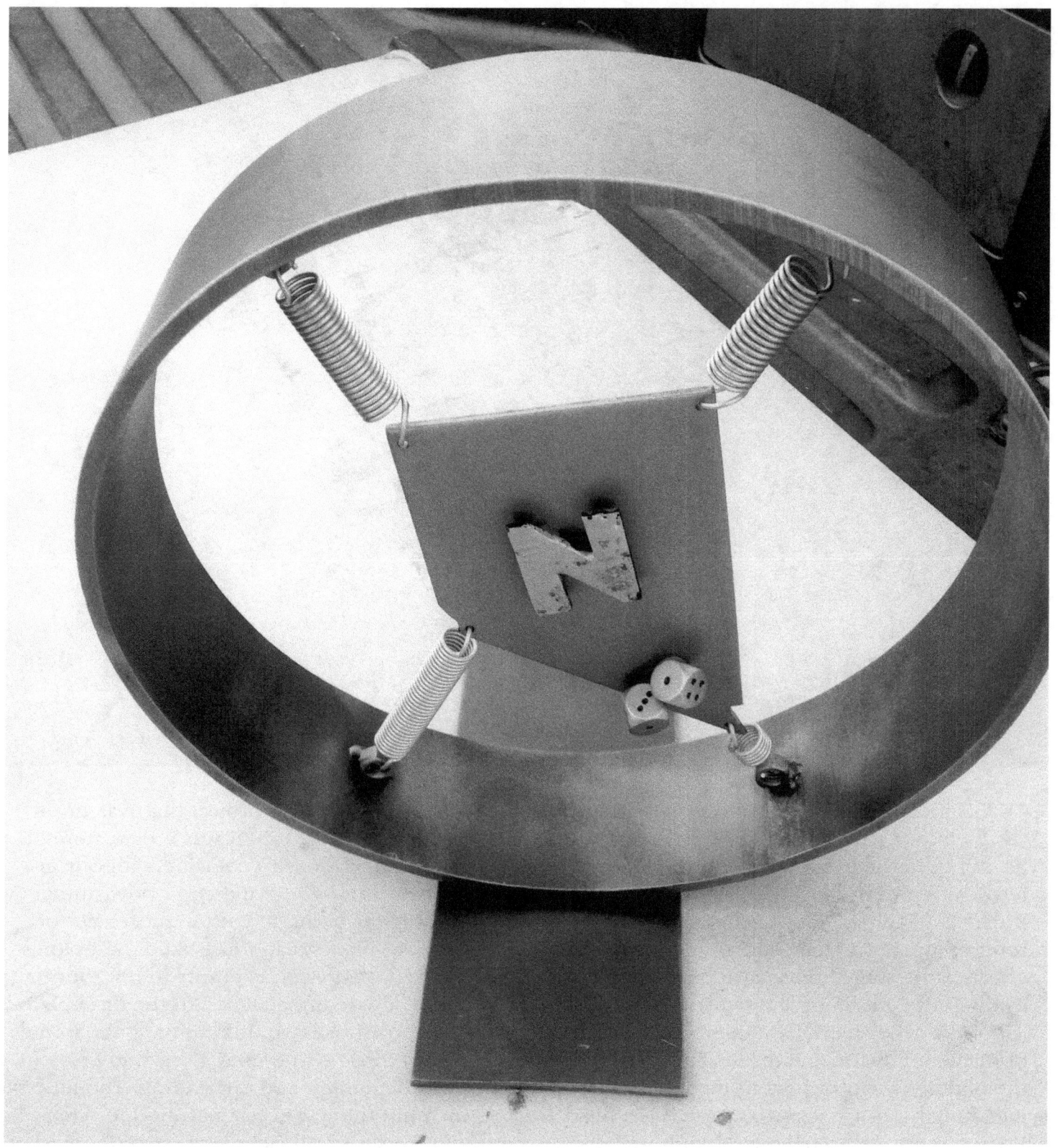

I never sold this piece but it was fun to build. I have no special connection to Nevada but I do remember finding the metal dice for sale on Amazon and that kind of inspired me to do the Nevada piece.

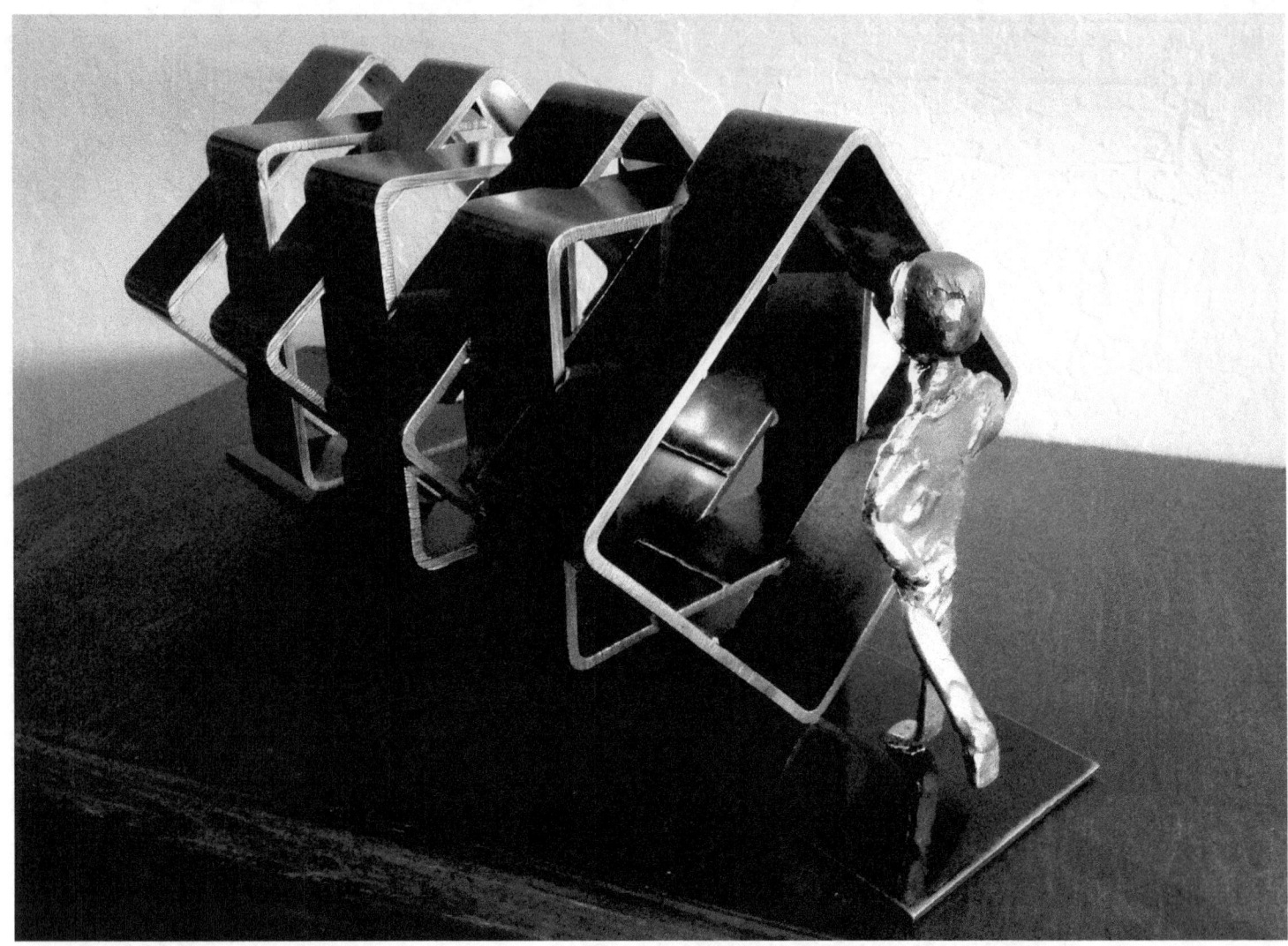

This piece is very special to me and in part came about from a writing project that was given us in our writing group. A picture of a tunnel was shown to the group. It was a dark tunnel having the bright light of day at the end. We were to write a short story to coincide with our interpretation of the picture. We often hear that phrase…"There is a light at the end of the tunnel" It usually signifies hope at the end of our endeavor. At first I was going to cut the pieces out of round pipe, but I changed my mind and went with the square pipe stock. I just liked the oblong effect of the staggered square pieces and to me they signified the twists and turns in our journey through the tunnel of life. Only the first square and the last square are attached to the base plate. All of the other pieces are interconnected and held in place by those two. It kind of spoke to me of birth and death, and the strong connection we all have to those two events. Everything else in the middle is sort of held in place by the grounding of our beginning and our ending. The little metal man was a hoot to construct! His head is a one inch nut that I had lying around to which I had no purpose. Somehow a "nut-head" just seemed to make sense. His legs were two old pieces of hardware from some cabinets that were demoed ten years ago. With an attitude very much like my fathers, I just always felt that there would be some use for them! Little did I know ten years ago that they would end up being the legs on the little man who is walking to the light at the end of the tunnel. For some reason, as I was bronzing the legs and body, I decided to not do his head. I just decided to leave it the natural metal. I like how his head is slightly lifted. To me it is his anticipation of the journey and positive outlook of what's ahead.

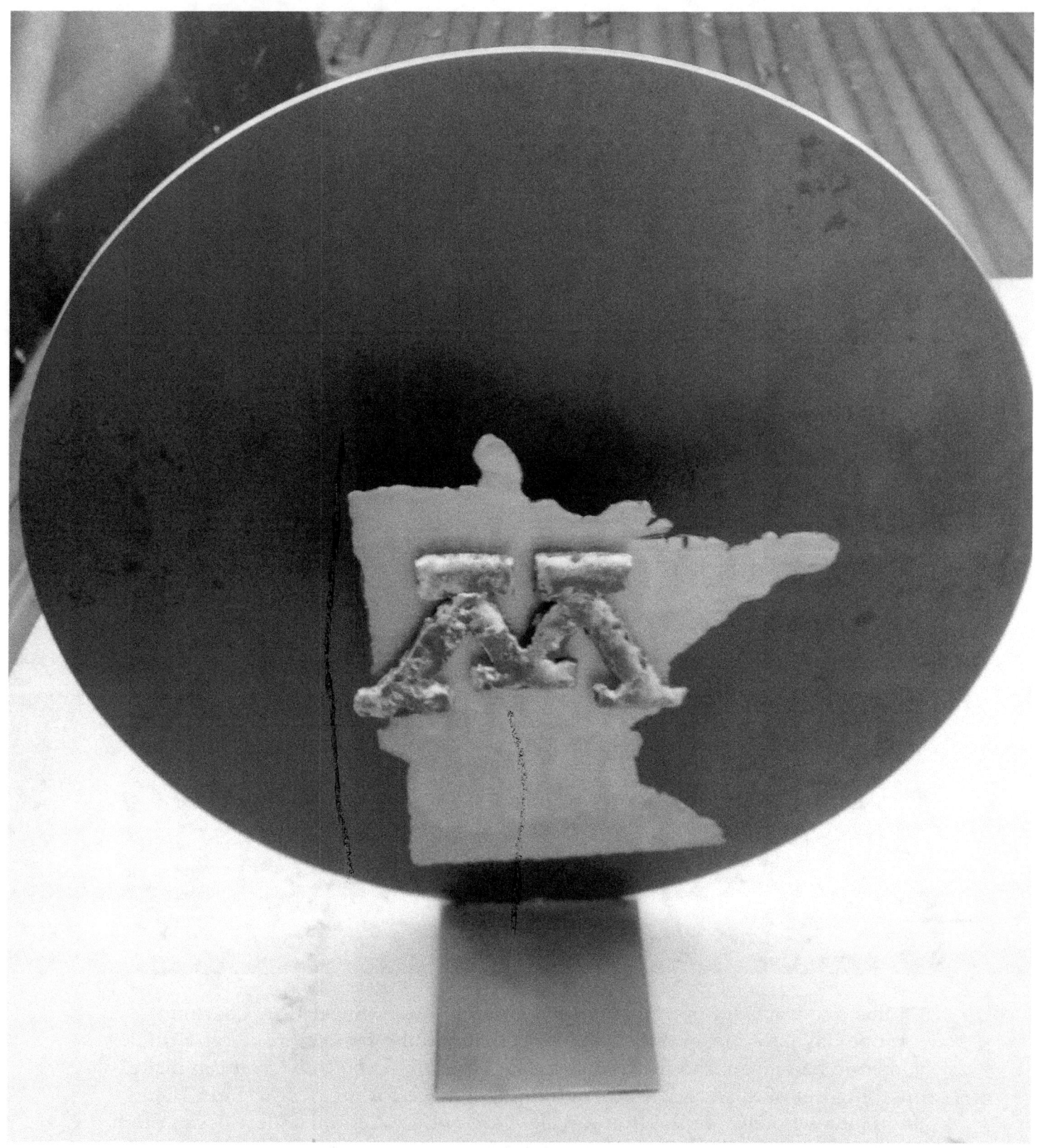

I did this piece for Eugene as well…Minnesota! I can't remember who was from Minnesota, maybe it was his dad? Anyway, I remember Gene saying that there was a room full of Minnesota stuff where this piece was going.

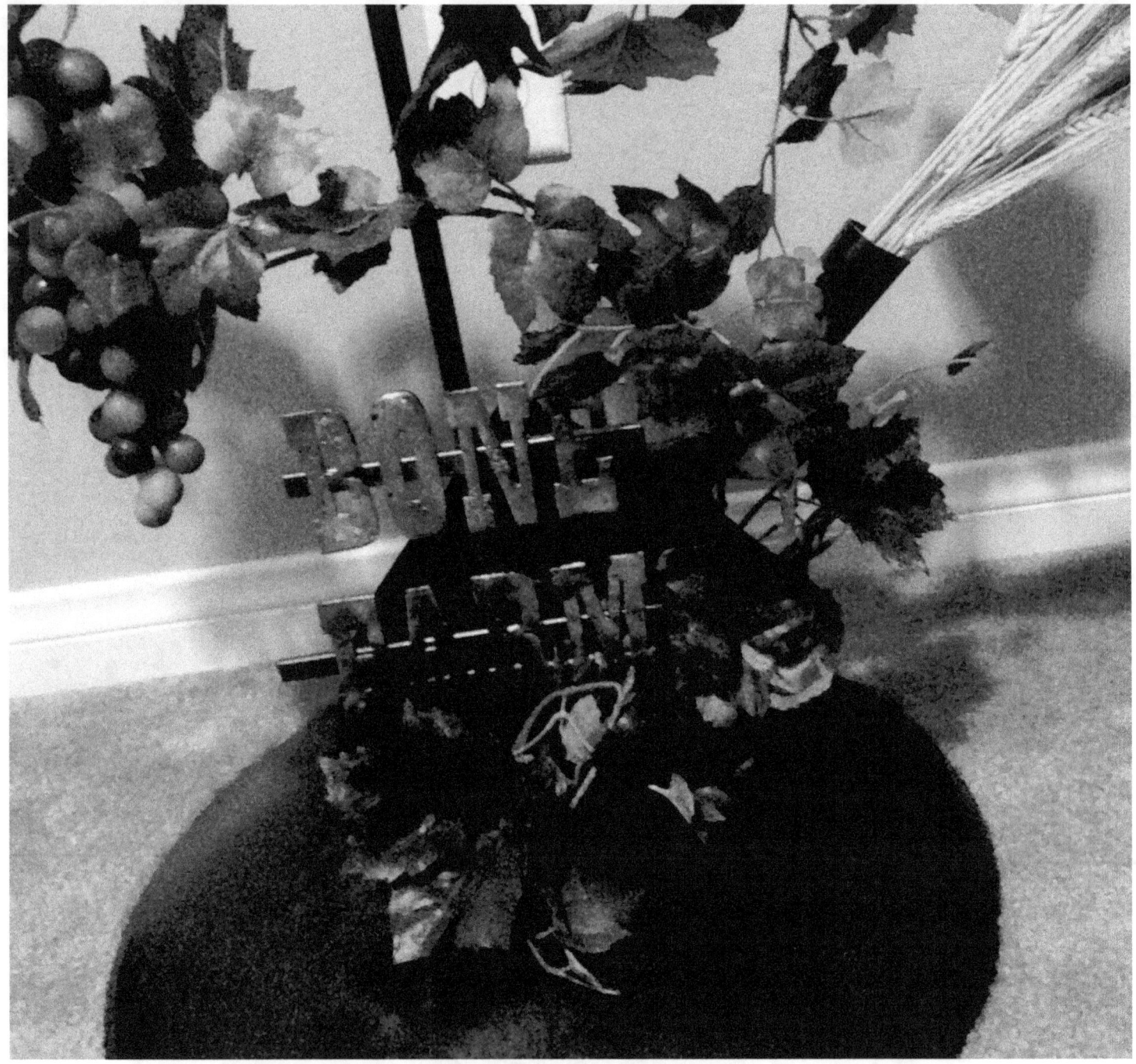

This one was a lot of fun! My friend and amazing artist at BAA Charlotte, one day gave me an old shovel head that had the handle broke off. I think someone had given it to her and she asked me…"Do you think you can make anything out of this??" I started envisioning a piece for my dear friends, Bryan and Linda who farm in the Buttonwillow area of the Central Valley. Bryan often gives me bags of almonds at harvest time which I enjoy making somewhat un-healthy with sea salt and honey, and then roasting them to a crispy brown delicious snack! They also grow grapes, pistachios and more. I buried the old shovel into an old plow blade that Don Preslar had given me, and then built the trellis out of ½" flat stock and mounted the "BONE FARMS" in bronzed metal letters. The fake grapes and grape leaves were courtesy of Beverly's Craft store in downtown Bako. Also, there are wheat stocks sticking out of what is left of the old shovel handle!

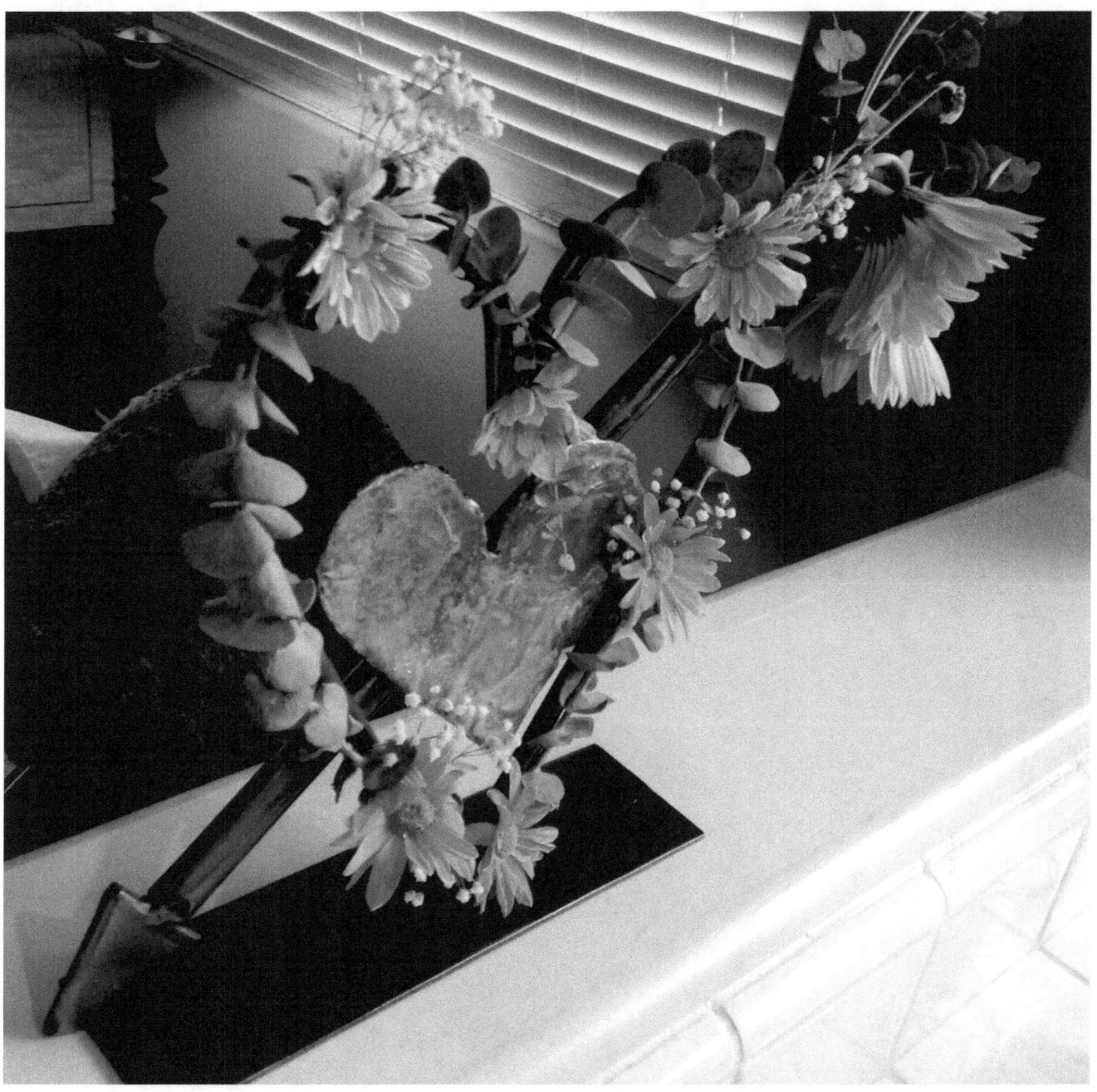

I made this piece for my beautiful wife, Brenda I think for her birthday. I then redid the flower display…or actually Conroy's in Bakersfield did it, and I gave it to her again for Valentine's Day! It was a hit both times. The heart is ½" round stock hand bent after heating with my torch. The arrow was a re-purposed piece of electrical conduit pipe. The arrowhead was formed out of some extra pieces of scrap metal and I made the arrow feathers out of scrap copper battery cable pieces.

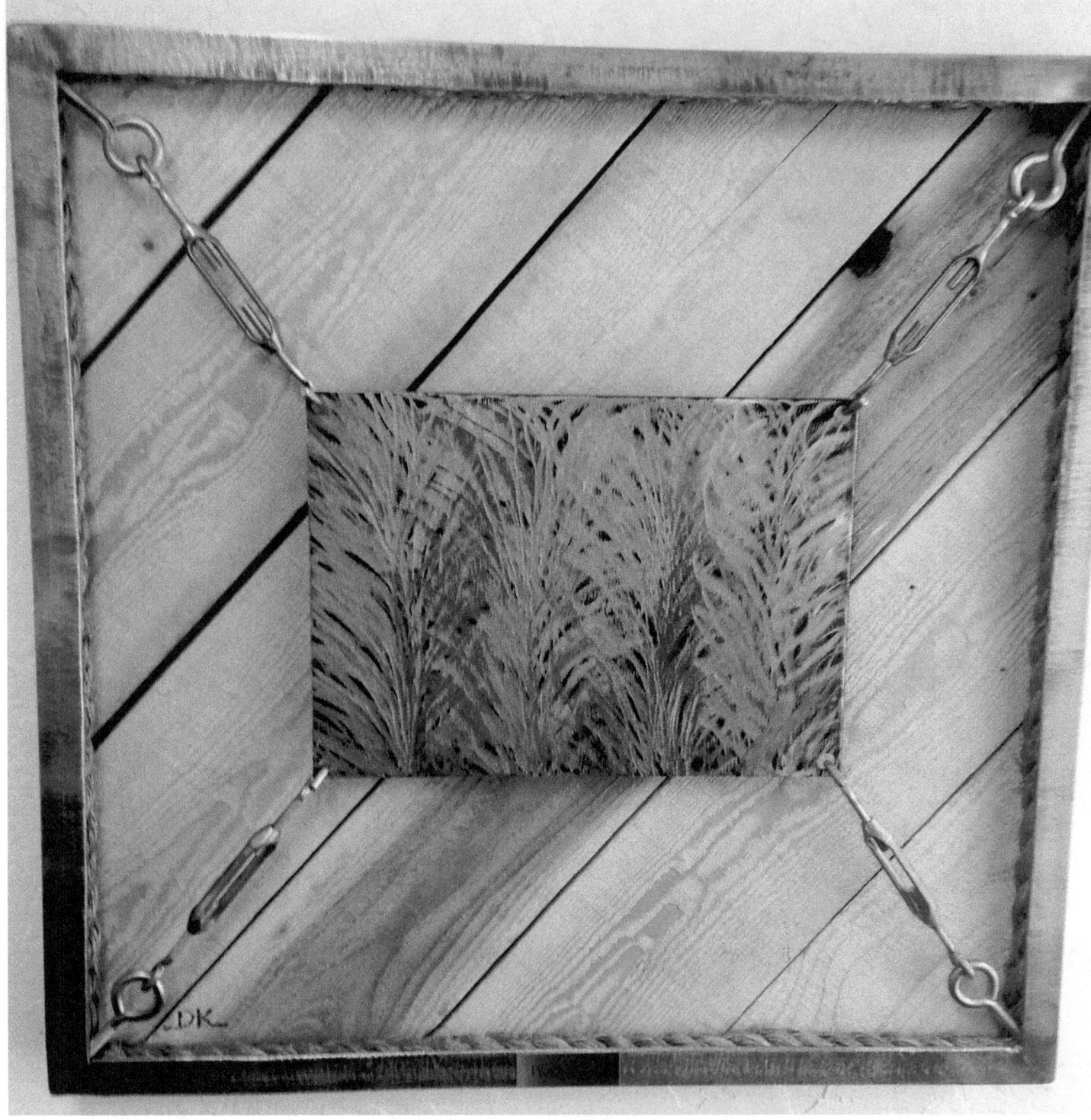

J ust sold this piece, Prairie Wind, in April 2016 to Julie who is an amazing artist member of The Bakersfield Art Association. It was on display there for a while and she always liked it and when she had the chance she made it her own! This piece is very special to me as it kind of got the whole thing started! We were in South Lake Tahoe to see our oldest son who is in the Navy and we had a day to kill while he was in training. We went to the shopping area right near the gondola that goes up the hill and we perused an art gallery. My attention was immediately taken to a display very similar to Prairie Wind and I thought to myself…"I could do that!" When I got home, I made this piece out of old used metal and oak shipping pallet wood. I think the name came from being a life-long Neil Young fan and I think Prairie Wind is a song he did many years ago.

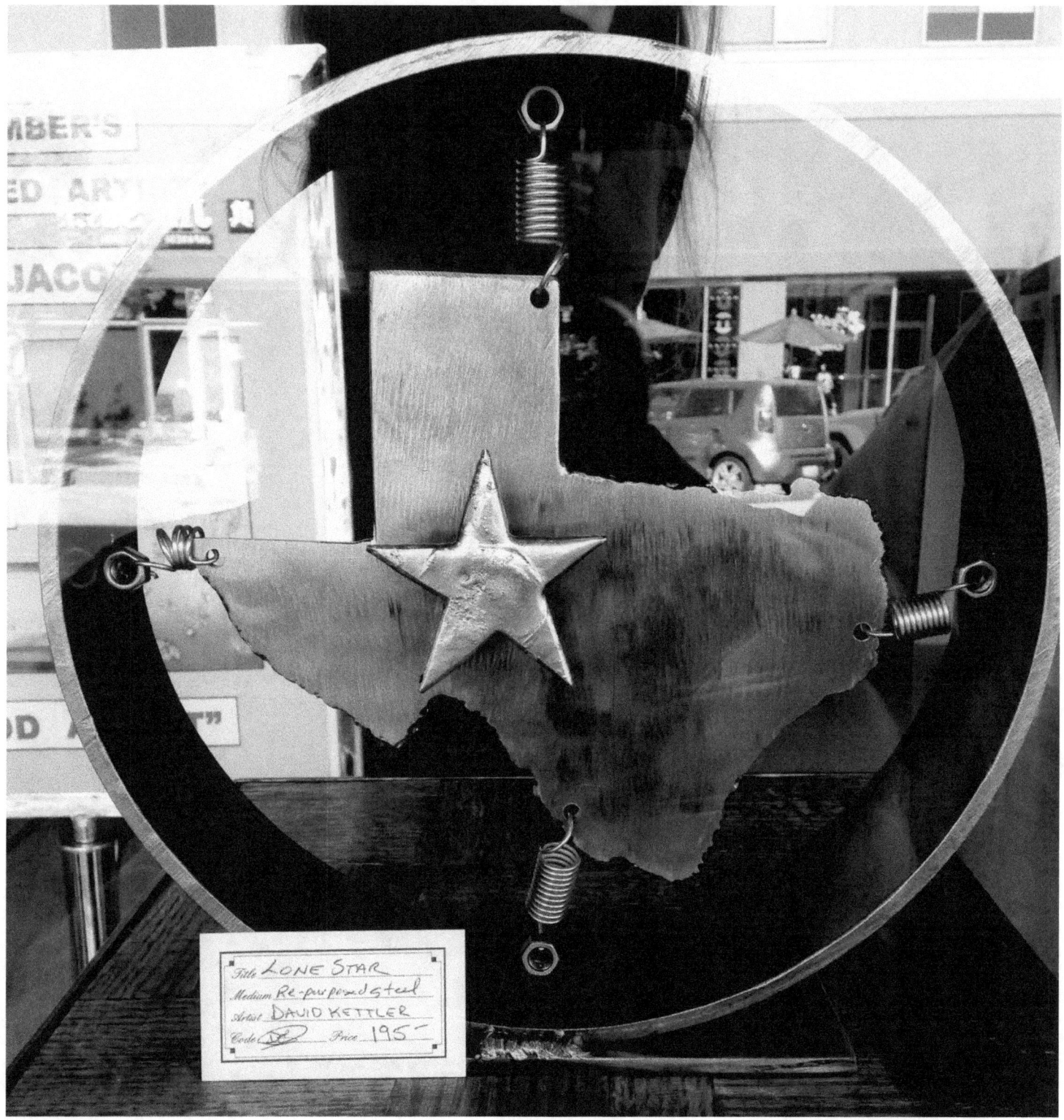

This is a piece that I did of Texas. I sold one of these and I made another one that I sent to Chip and JoAnne of Fixer Upper fame. They sent me a very nice thank you note that I really appreciated!

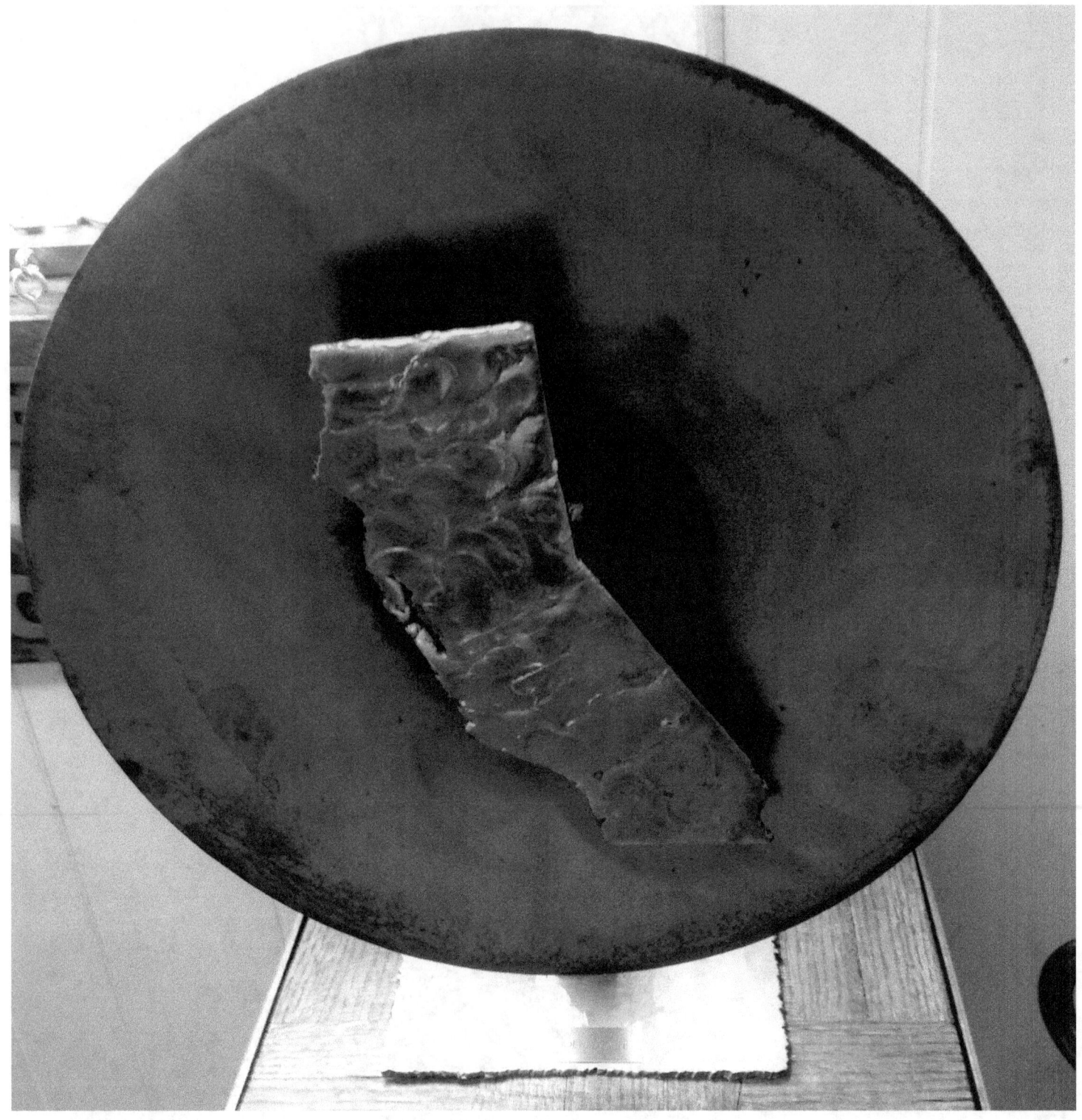

This is one of the very first metal pieces that I made using a state. I called it the "Golden State" and I sold a few of these.

Furniture

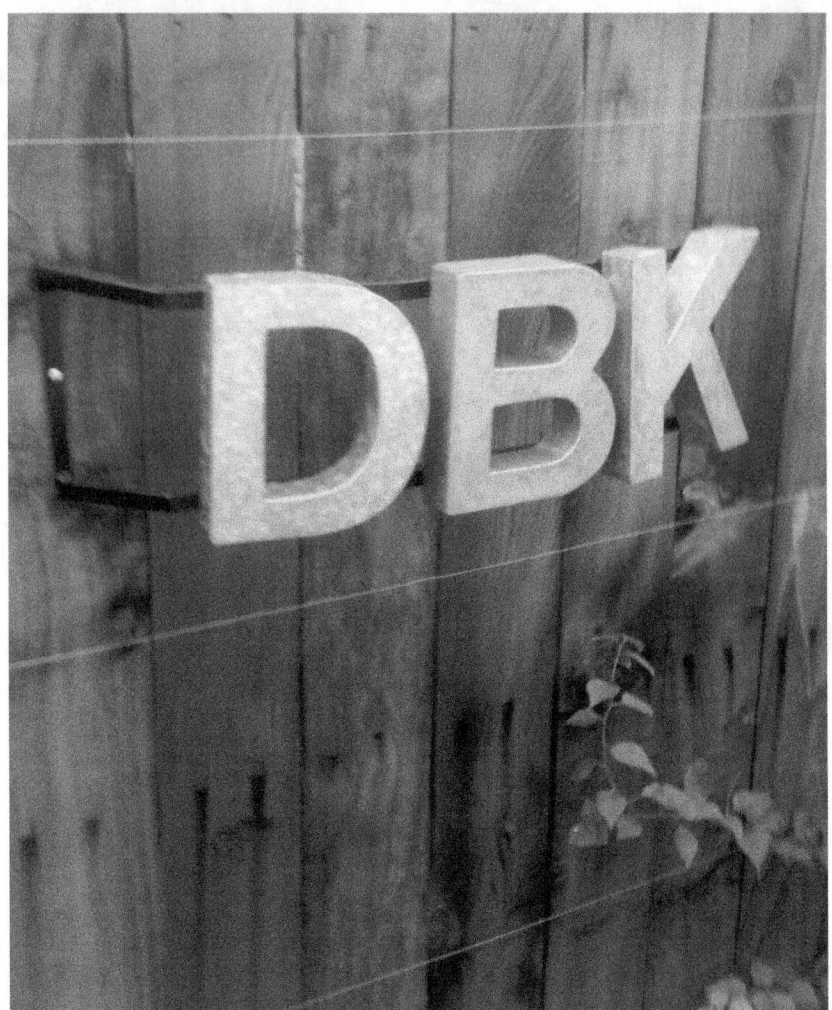

This is a sign that I made years ago that hangs on the fence just outside of our kitchen window. In the summer it is engulfed in Bougainvillea flowers and looks really neat. I did not make the tin letters, they can be purchased from Pottery Barn Catalog and then I just mounted them on a metal frame.

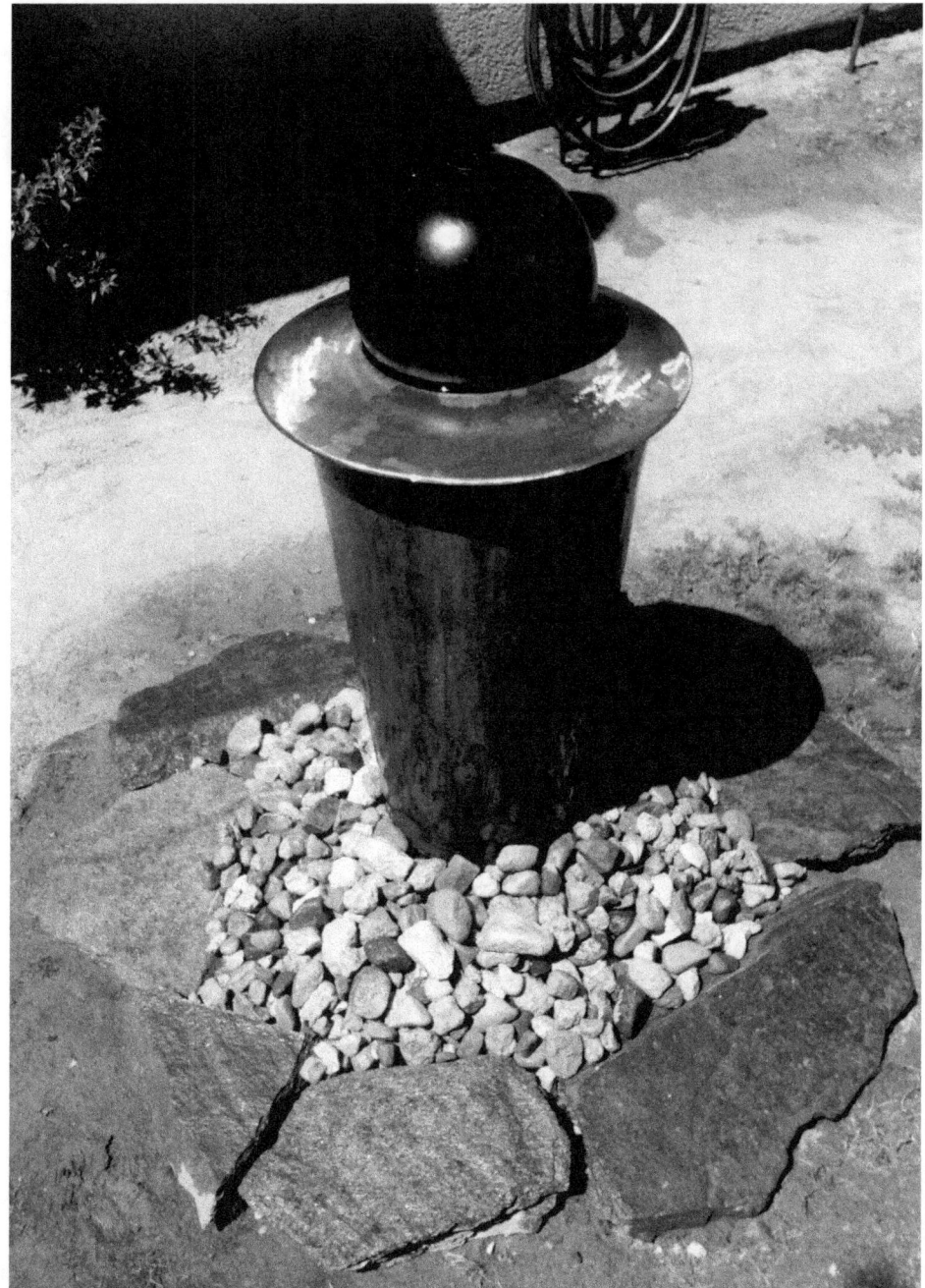

I wanted to build a fountain in our backyard so this is what I came up with. I started with a large ceramic jar and then I mounted an old plow disc on top with the middle cut out. The black ball was actually a part from a lamp and I just threaded the PVC pipe up through it where the water comes out. There is a cemented reservoir full of rocks and the water pump is down underneath the water. The pump is activated by a remote switch that also turns on the outside twinkle lights in the trees. It really works great and we enjoy it a lot especially in the summer.

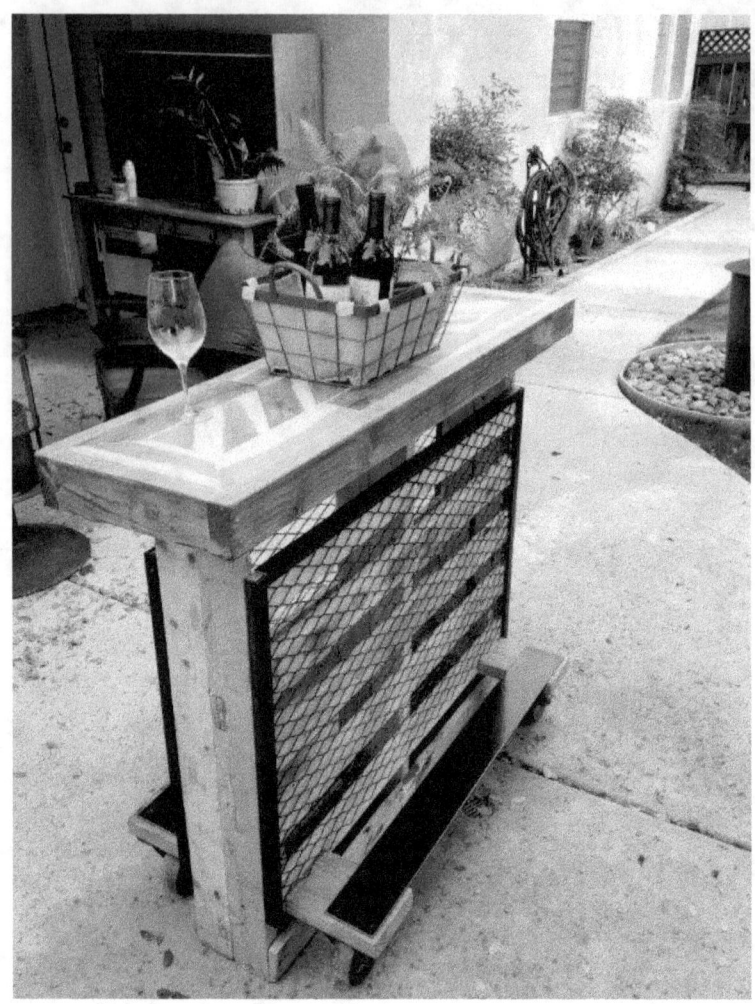

Brenda saw a similar table made out of old shipping pallets so I thought I would give it a try. The old metal casters came from my friend Bob England, and the rest is just re-purposed metal and two by fours along with the pallets. It is entering its second go-around seeing that the rain and dampness caused the table top to swell and crack. I rebuilt the top and now I'm mounting a glass piece on the top that will protect it from the rain. It really is meant to be an outside piece.

The story of Robert L.

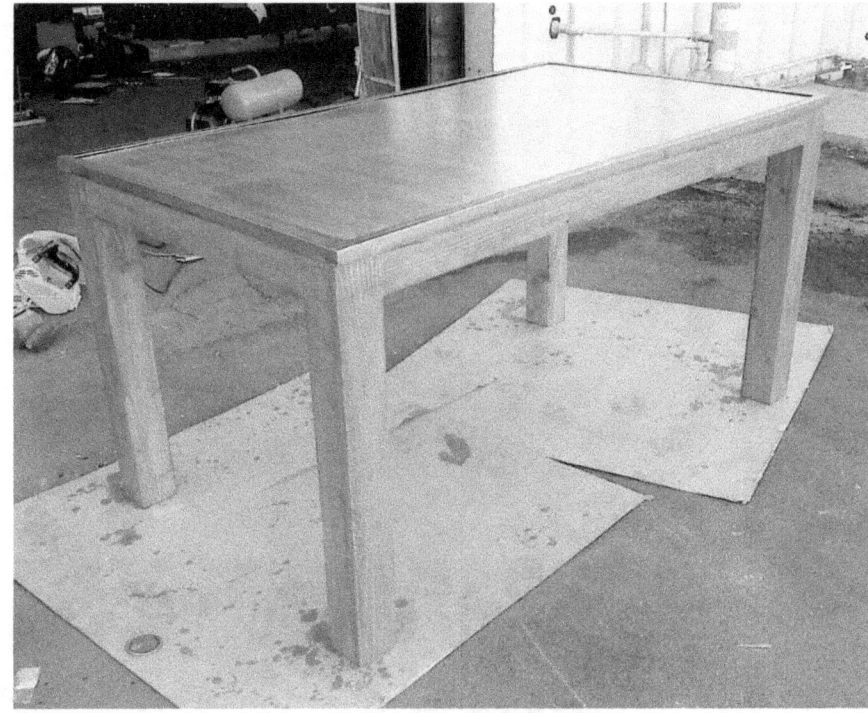

This picture of our dining room table always reminds me of Robert. I was working one evening on my dining room table in the alley behind our shop. I had often seen this guy who rode around on a bicycle with a small trailer in tow that carried two beagle dogs. It appeared that he was probably homeless and this one day I was kind of irritated because he came up the alley and stopped. I just knew he was going to ask me for some money. He got off his bike and came over to where I was working and exclaimed…"Man, what a beautiful table…Are you making that!?" Now that my entire opinion of him changed in an instant, he had my total attention. "Why yes I proclaimed with bursting pride!"

We continued small talk for a while, learned each other's names, and I petted his very friendly dogs. Off he rode down the alley and my thought was, what a nice guy! A few days later, Robert came by and asked if I would keep an eye on his dogs for just a bit while he went to put his name in at the employment place in order to try and get a job. This was shock number three. First of all, here is a homeless guy who thinks about and complements someone else's efforts, Secondly he takes amazing care of his animals even while being homeless and thirdly, he wants to go try and get a job.

I did not mind watching the dogs at all, they were really cool dogs! However, the one started HOWLING the minute Robert left on his bicycle and did not stop until he returned! True love! Every time Robert came around, we talked more and more. I learned that he was a U.S. Marine Veteran who spent twenty years stationed at Camp Pendleton down south where my best friend Randy's dad was stationed. I found out that he was a certified welder back East and had a driver's license from some state on the East Coast. He had gone through a bad divorce and just kind of checked out of life. He told me he never drank alcohol and I never smelled it on him so alcoholism didn't seem to be the problem.

Later, Robert again asked me to keep an eye on his dogs while he rode to the DMV and got his driver's license transferred to California. To make a long story short….Robert ended up getting TWO jobs…one was a night watchman of some commercial property where he and his dogs could stay with some security and a restroom. He then got a job welding during the day that paid $10 per hour. Robert got his California driver's license, he paid cash for an old beater car, showed me the certificate that proved he had put insurance on it, and eventually…Robert bought a small mobile home in Lake Isabella.

I don't see Robert very often anymore but he will always remain one of my heroes in life. To come from where he found himself, and with all that was against him, to continue to strive and improve while always having a great attitude and a big smile have many days encouraged me! It all started with a genuine complement…."Man, that table you're building is beautiful!"

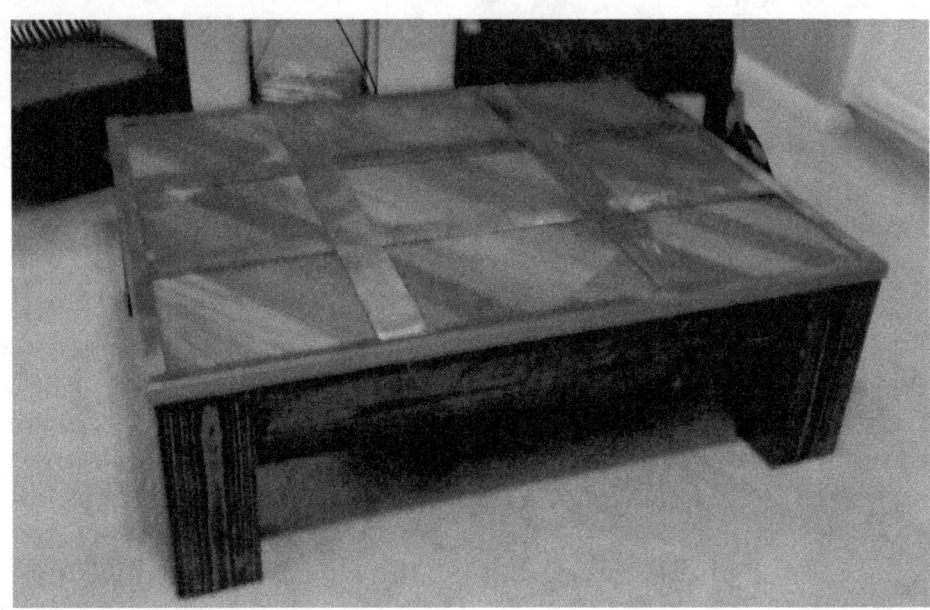

This is a coffee table that I built a while back for our den. I ended up selling it because it was a bit too big for our new house. It was constructed of two by four's, four by four's with wood flooring used for the top. I built a metal framework around it for aesthetics.

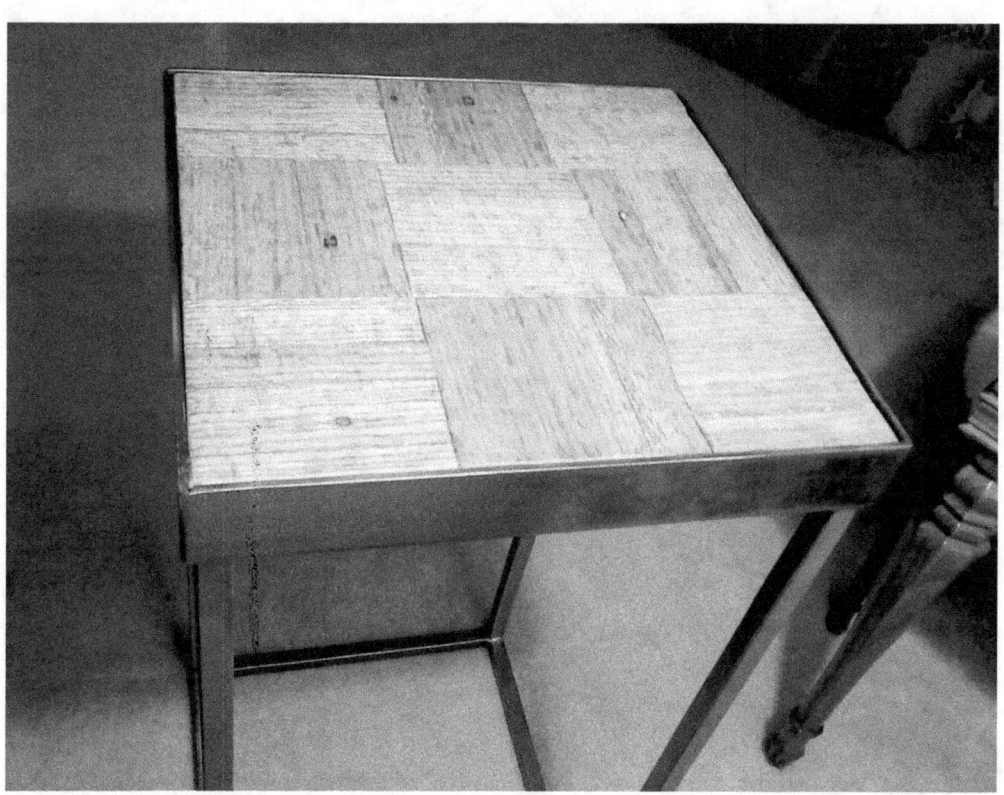

I built this end table which graced the side of my big leather chair for many years. The top is a pattern of old pallet wood set in a framework of angle iron. It received a couple revisions over the years and recently I sold it to my friend Stan.

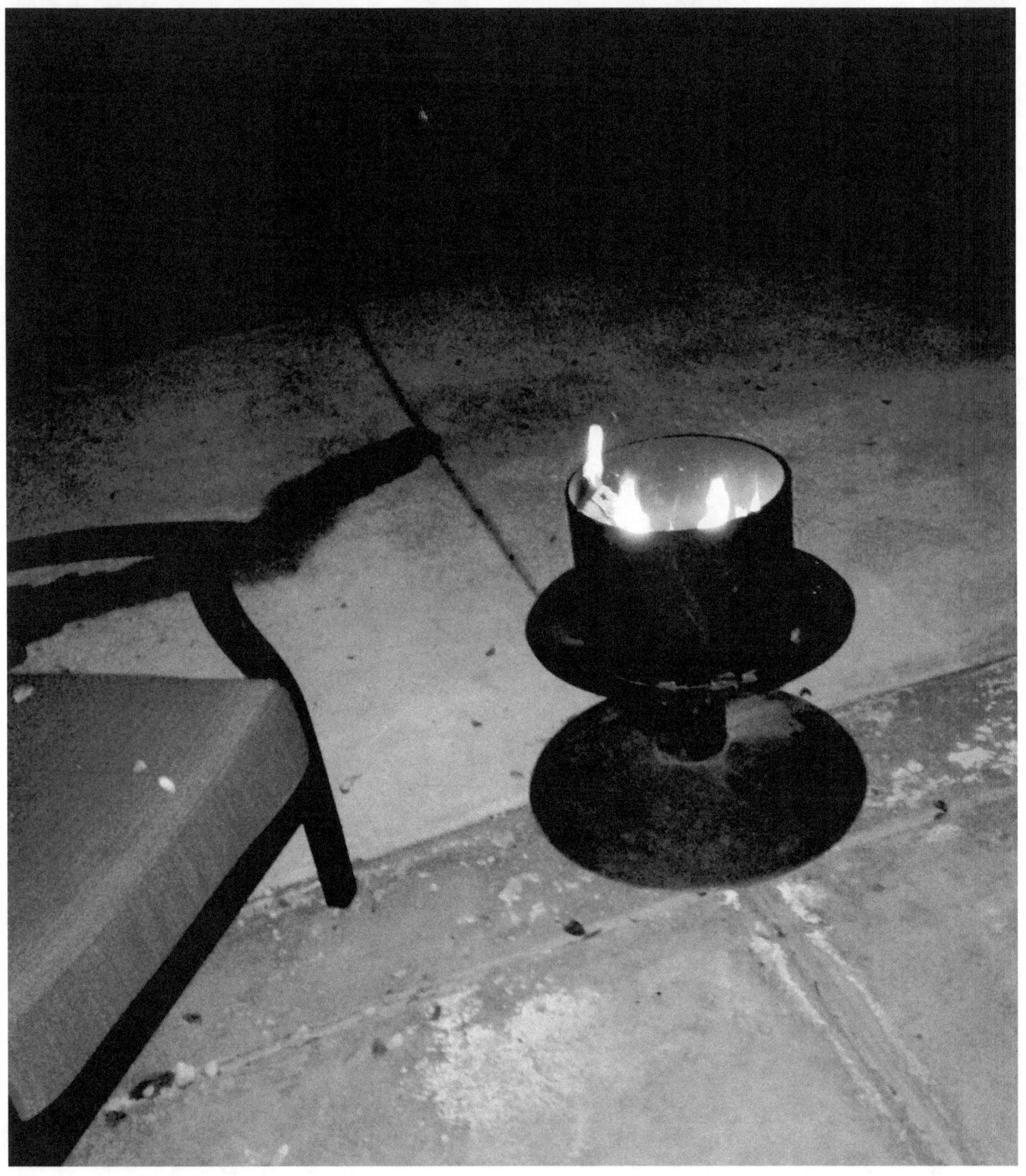

When Jim's Supply cuts pipe for me, they can only go so far and what was left over from the scrap piece that Don gave me was about a foot long. I decided to mount it on plow discs and make a fire pit for our back yard. As long as we have legal burn days in the winter, it works great.

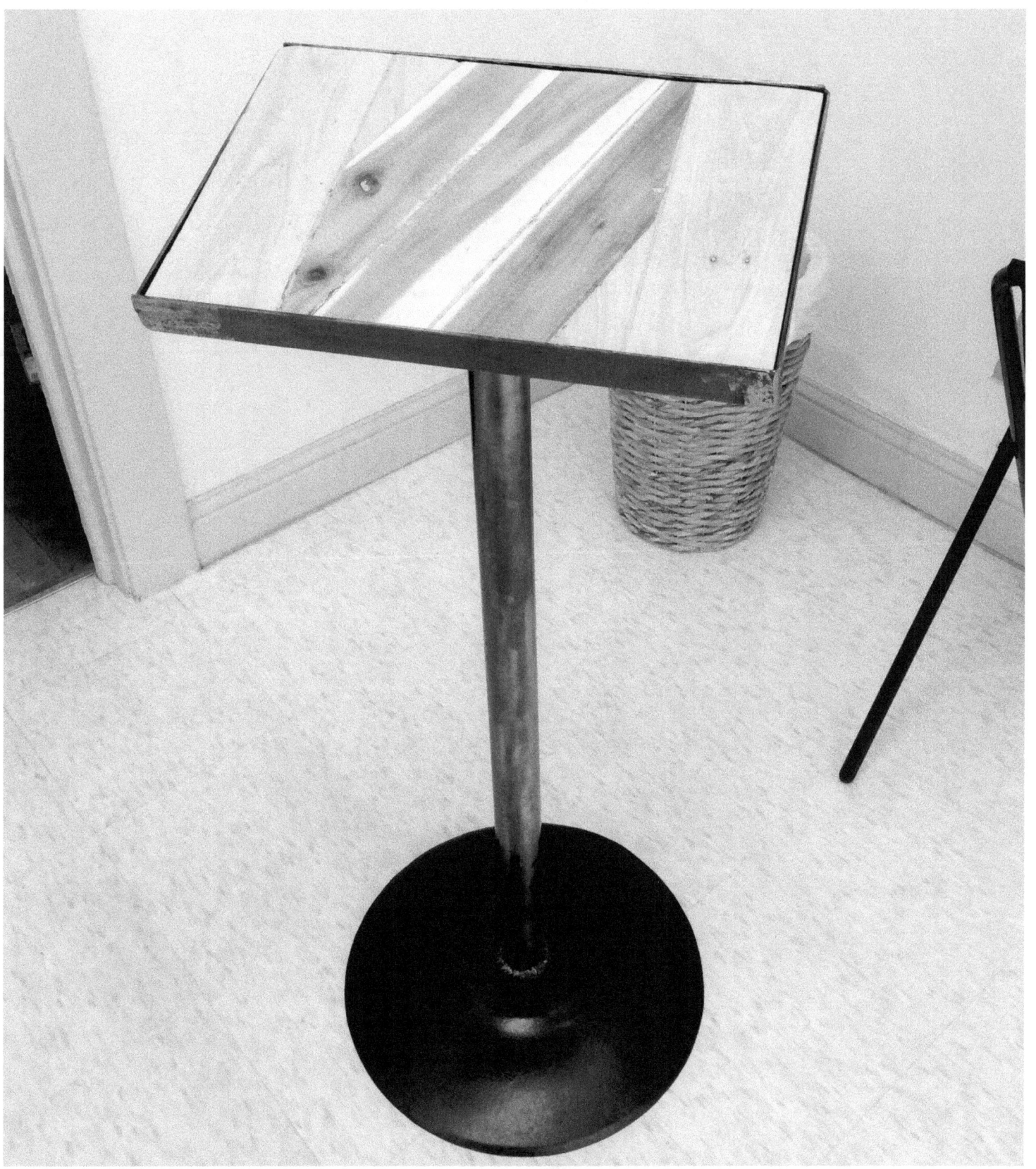

My friend Toni at the Art Center had asked me if I could build a podium for the instructors to use when they taught their art classes…could I ever!! The only problem is everything that I build is really heavy!! They sometimes have issues transporting the thing to its proper place of usefulness! I used an old plow disc, some repurposed pipe and some old shipping pallet hard-wood. It turned out really beautiful and was a big hit.

Planters

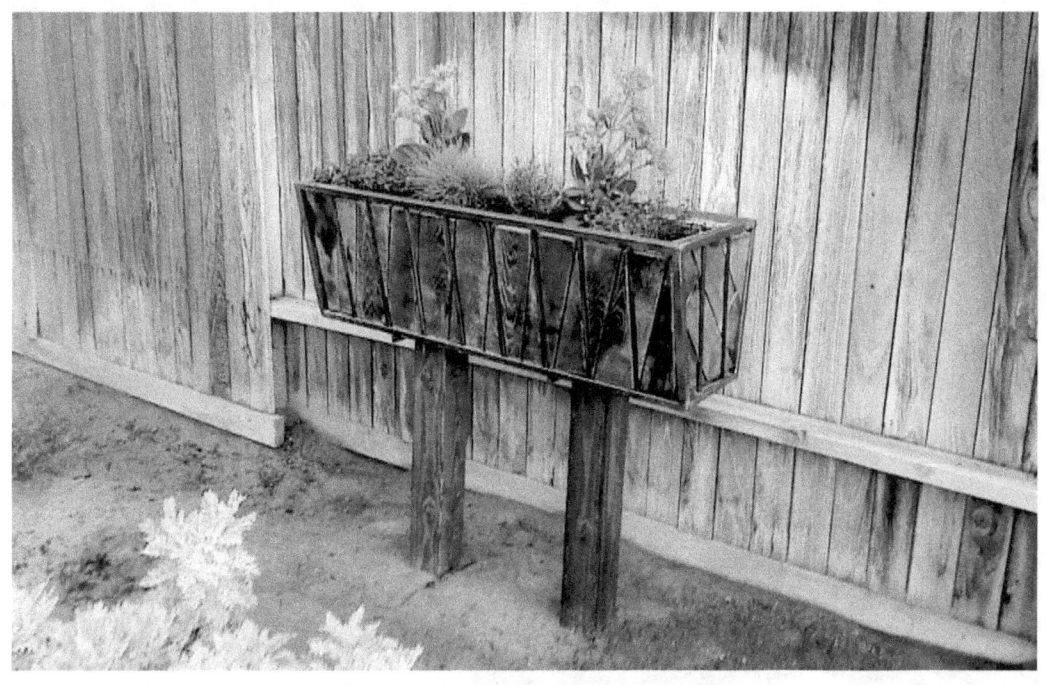

I built this a number of years ago out of old oak shipping pallet wood and 1" square stock metal. I still have it. It stands in front of the battery shop on F Street in Bakersfield.

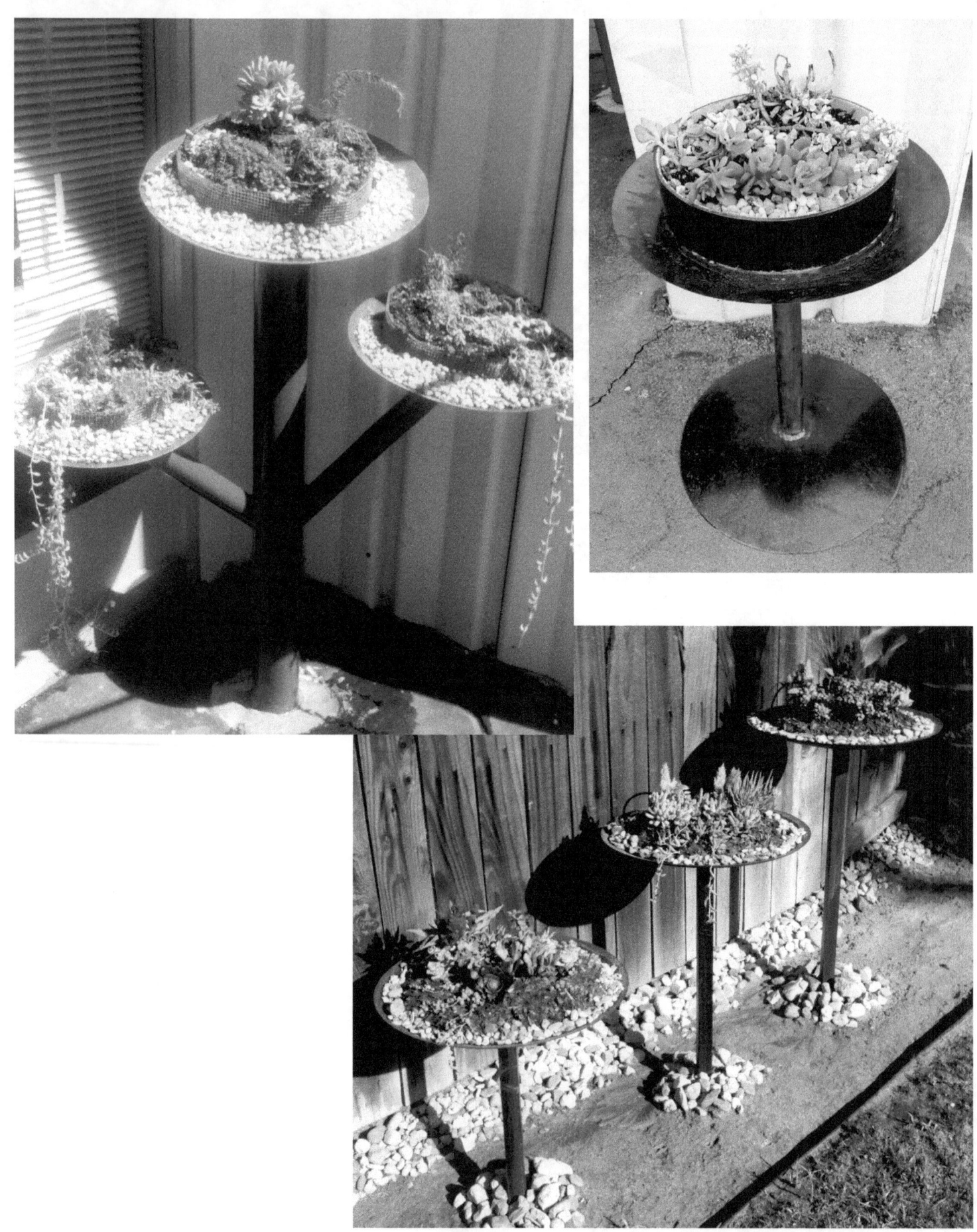

These are planters I made out of old plow disc's and re-purposed metal.
Some are in our back yard and some are at the battery shop.

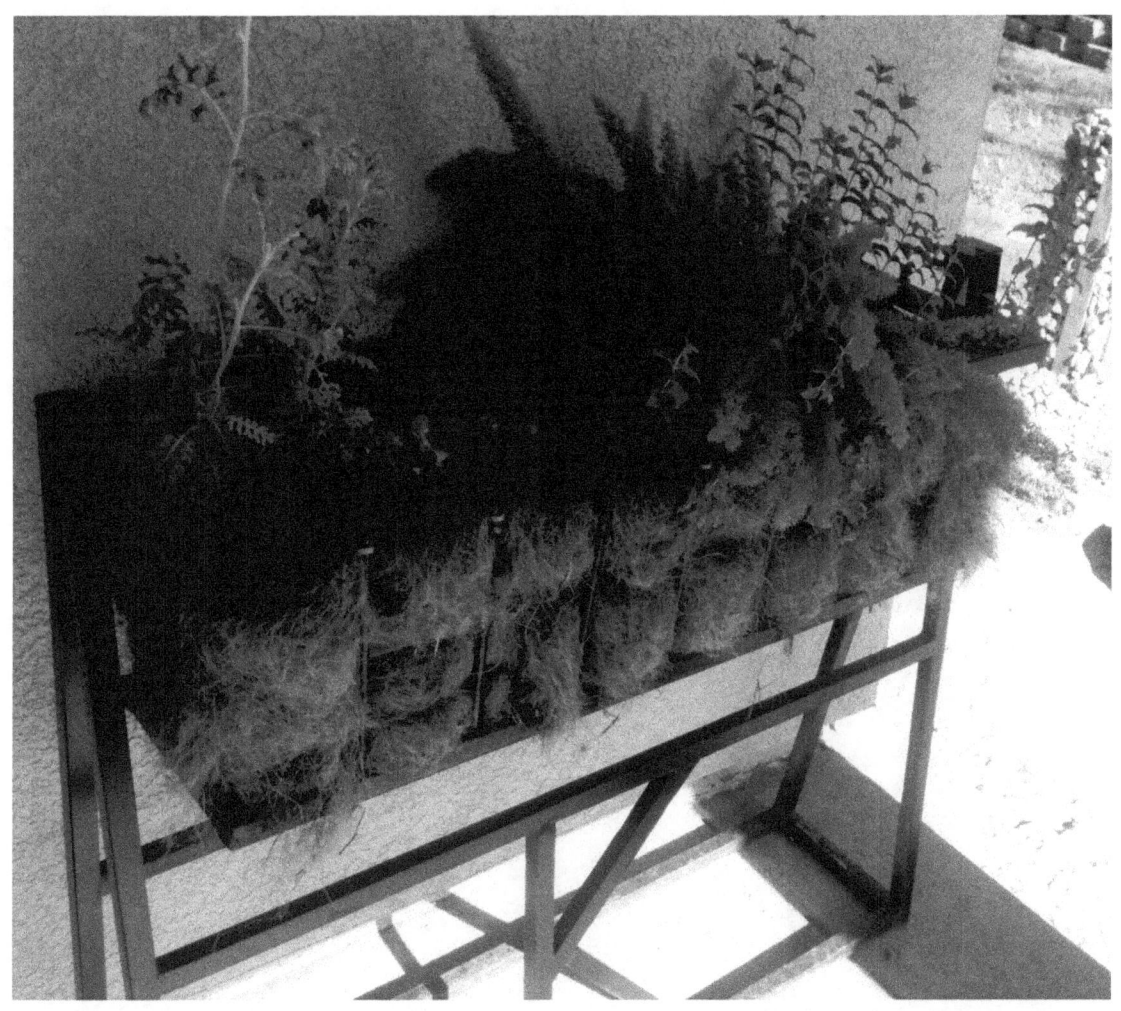

I built this for our front yard and we still have it! It sits in our back yard now and it is still filled with succulents.

Wine Bottle Jewelry

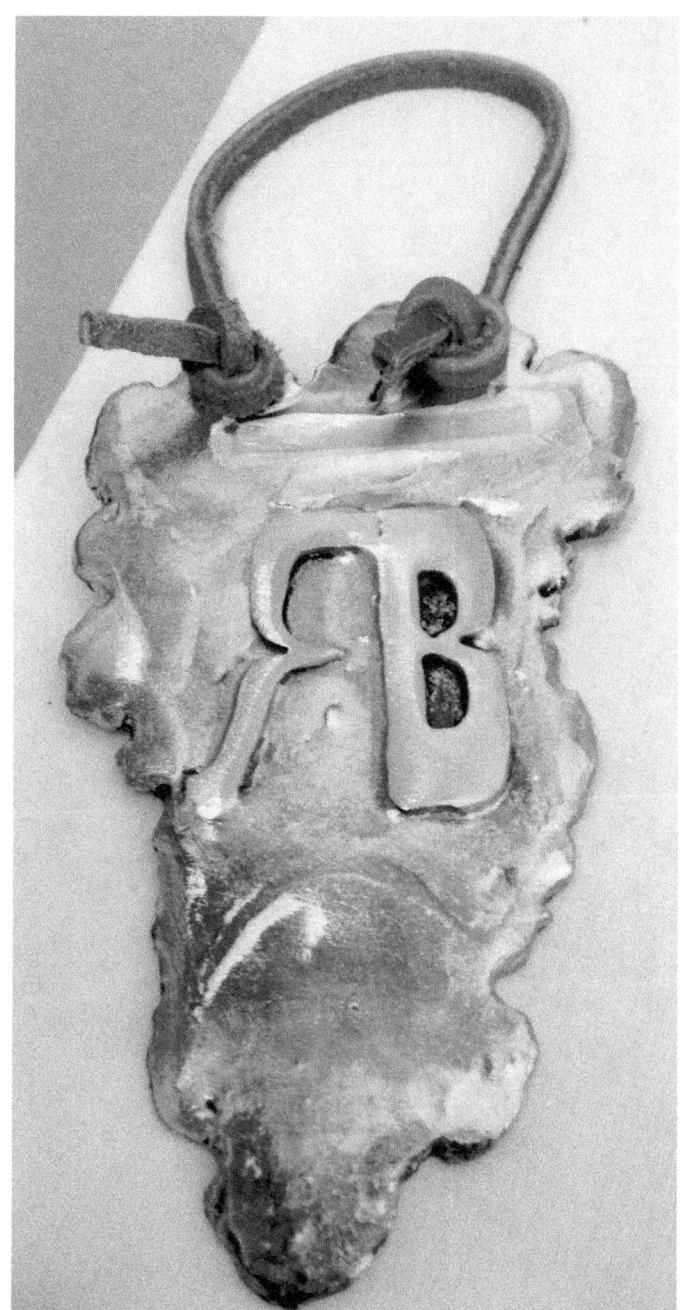

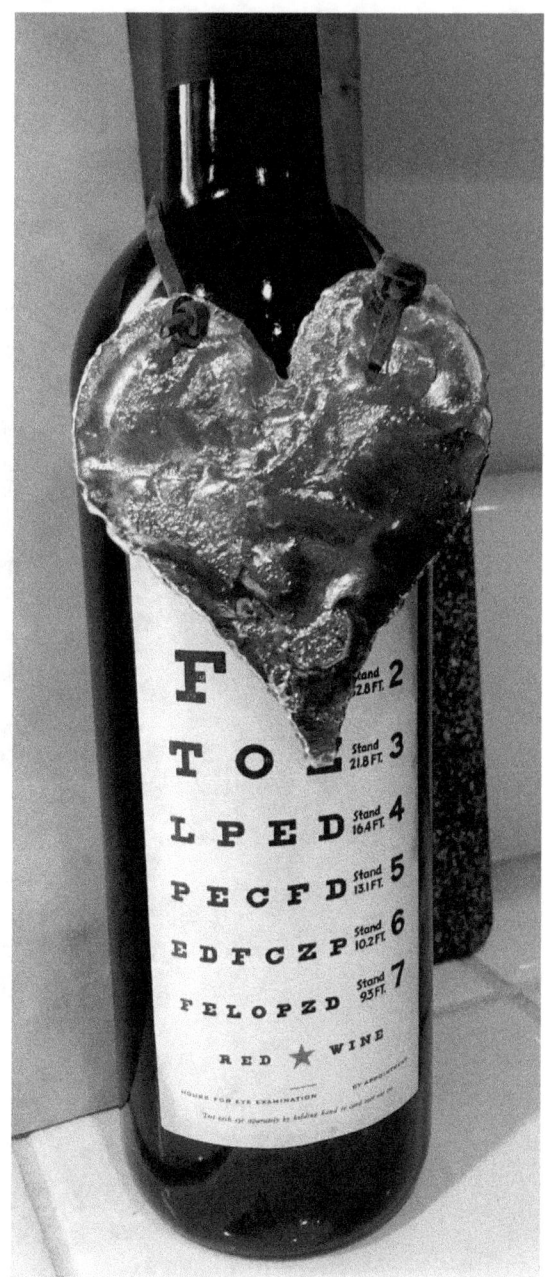

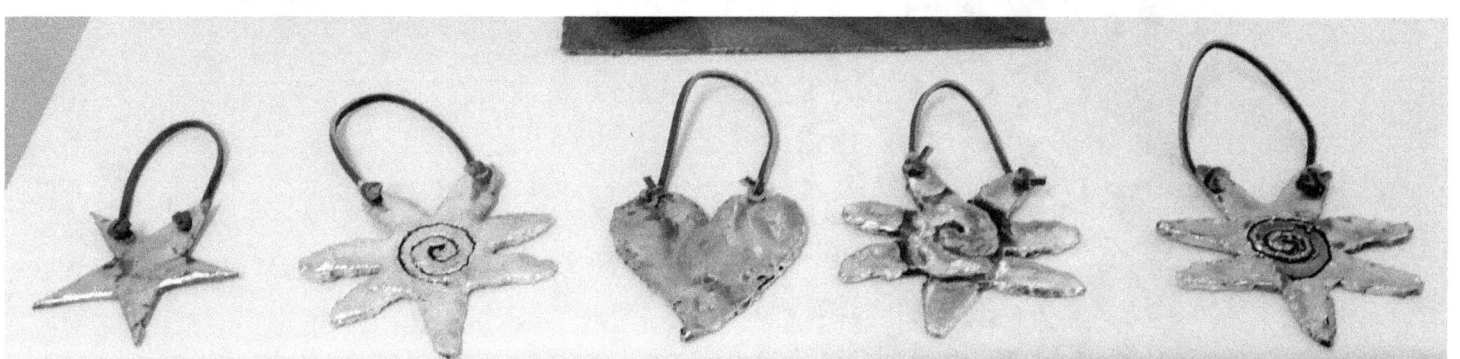

How this began was Brenda showed me a cool piece of ceramic that said... "Celebrate" on it and it was meant to hang around a wine bottle. I starting thinking about doing it out of metal and the first one I did was a heart. It's plate steel cut out with a hand torch and then covered in bronze. I have sold quite a few of them!

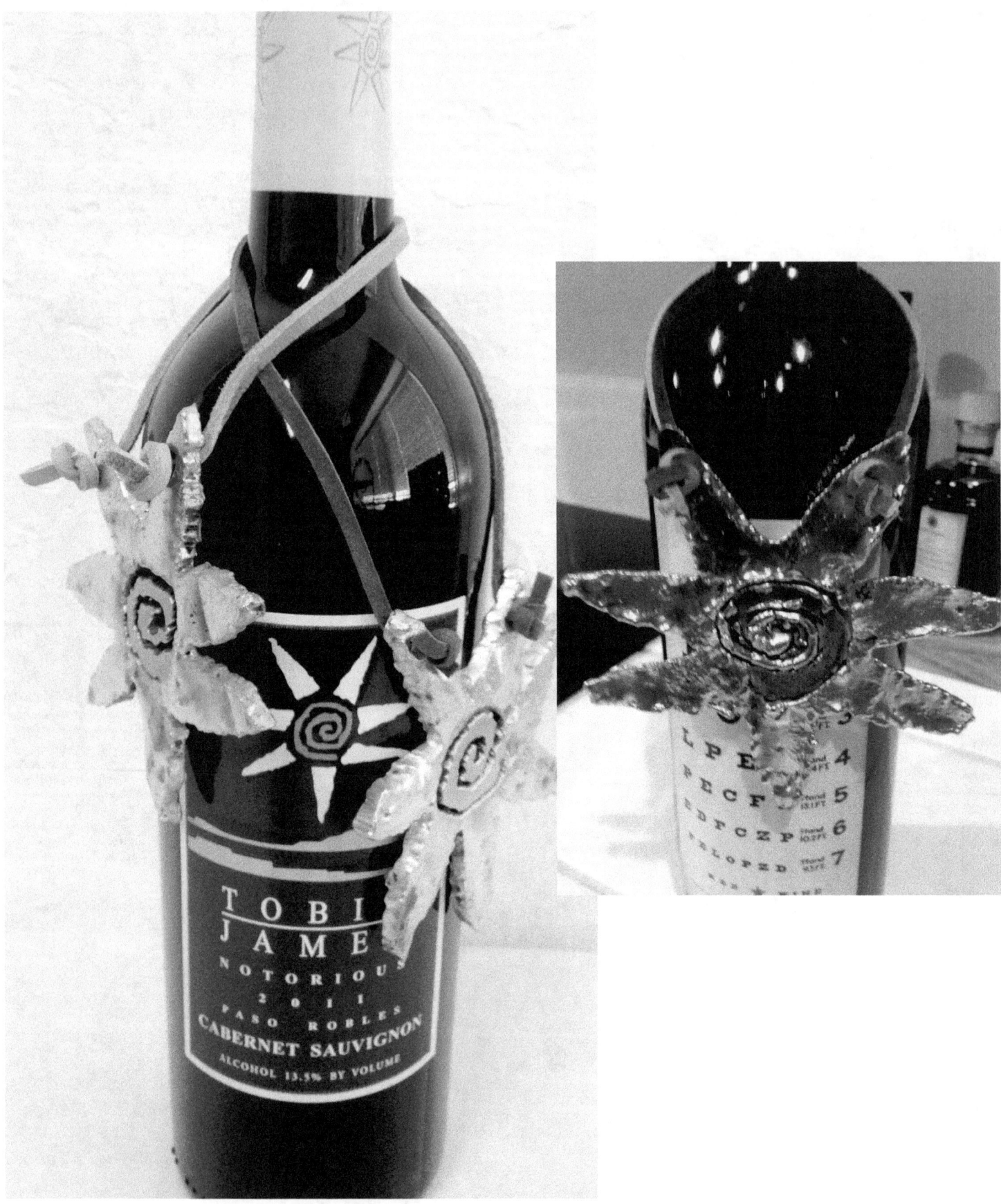

I sent out a few of my hearts to different wineries and the first one to contact me was a winery in Paso Robles. They wanted me to do one of their logo which is a specially constructed "sun" and I was able to re-create it and sent them some that they sell in their tasting room.

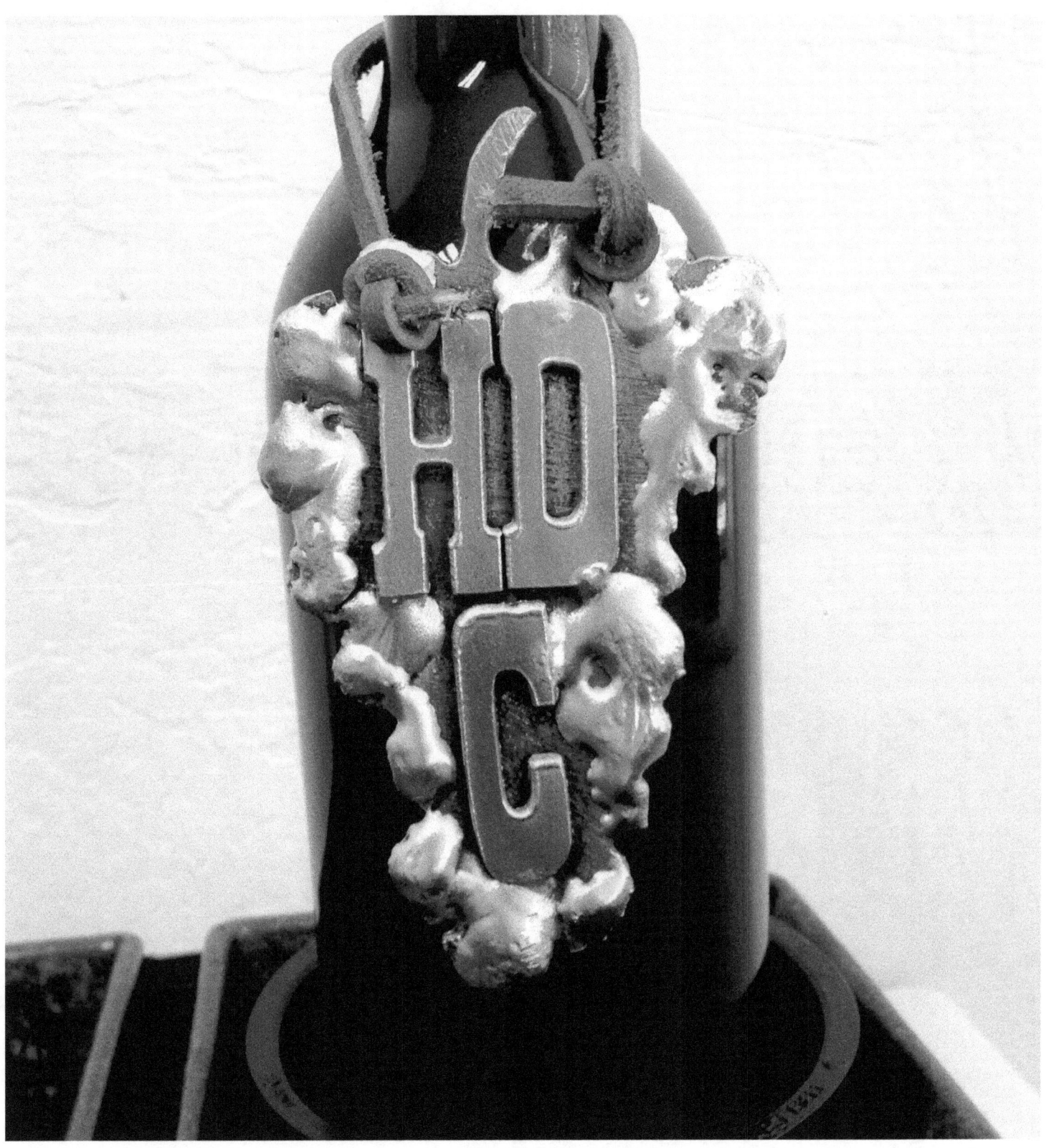

This was a cluster of grapes that I cut out and then bronzed the letters on it for a winery in Palmdale California.

Recognition Pieces

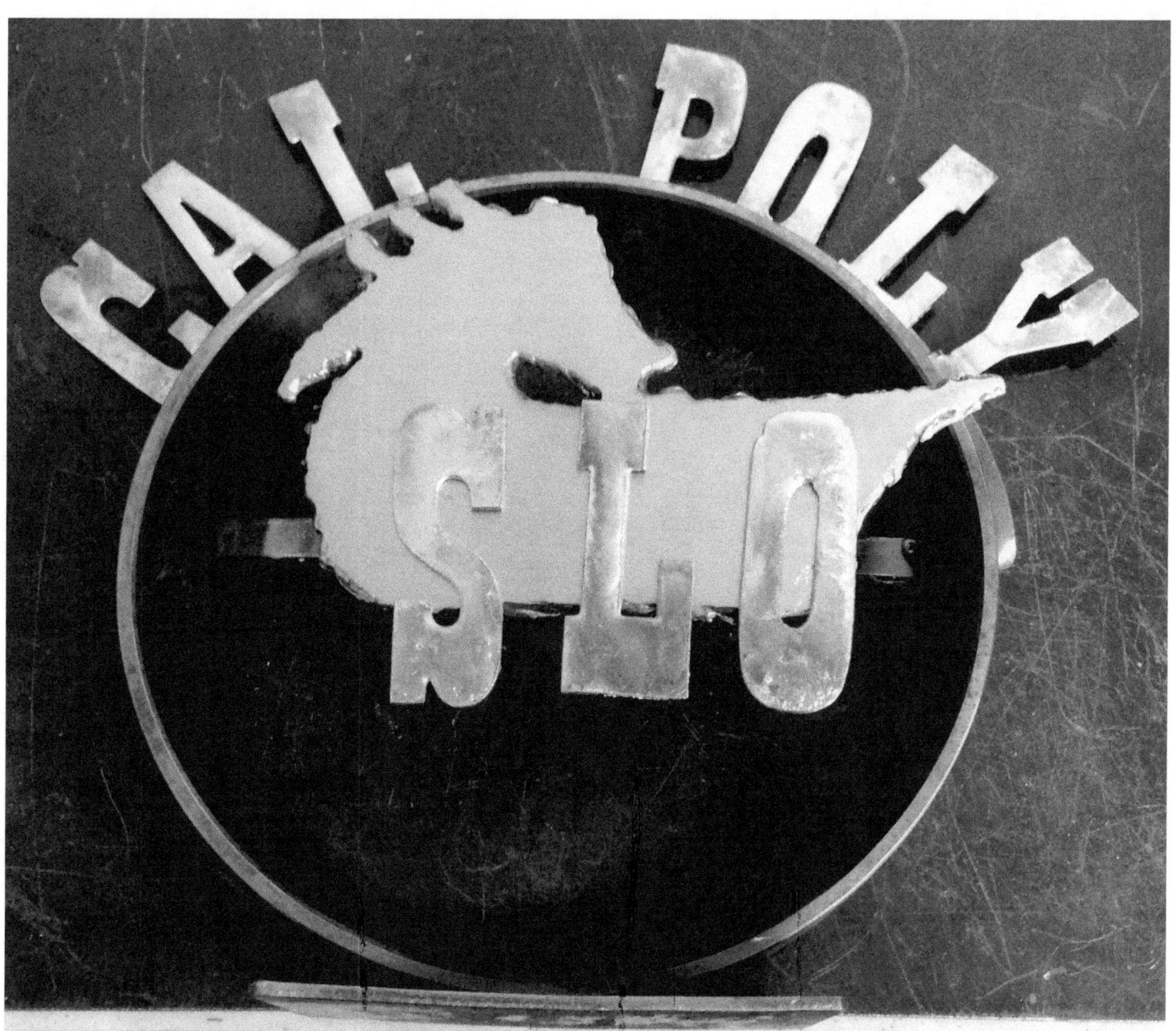

I did this piece for my middle son, Darren who graduated from Cal Poly SLO. I love their motto which is "Learn by doing." I practice that a lot in my metal art. I visualize and conceptualize, and then I just start the doing process and see where it leads.

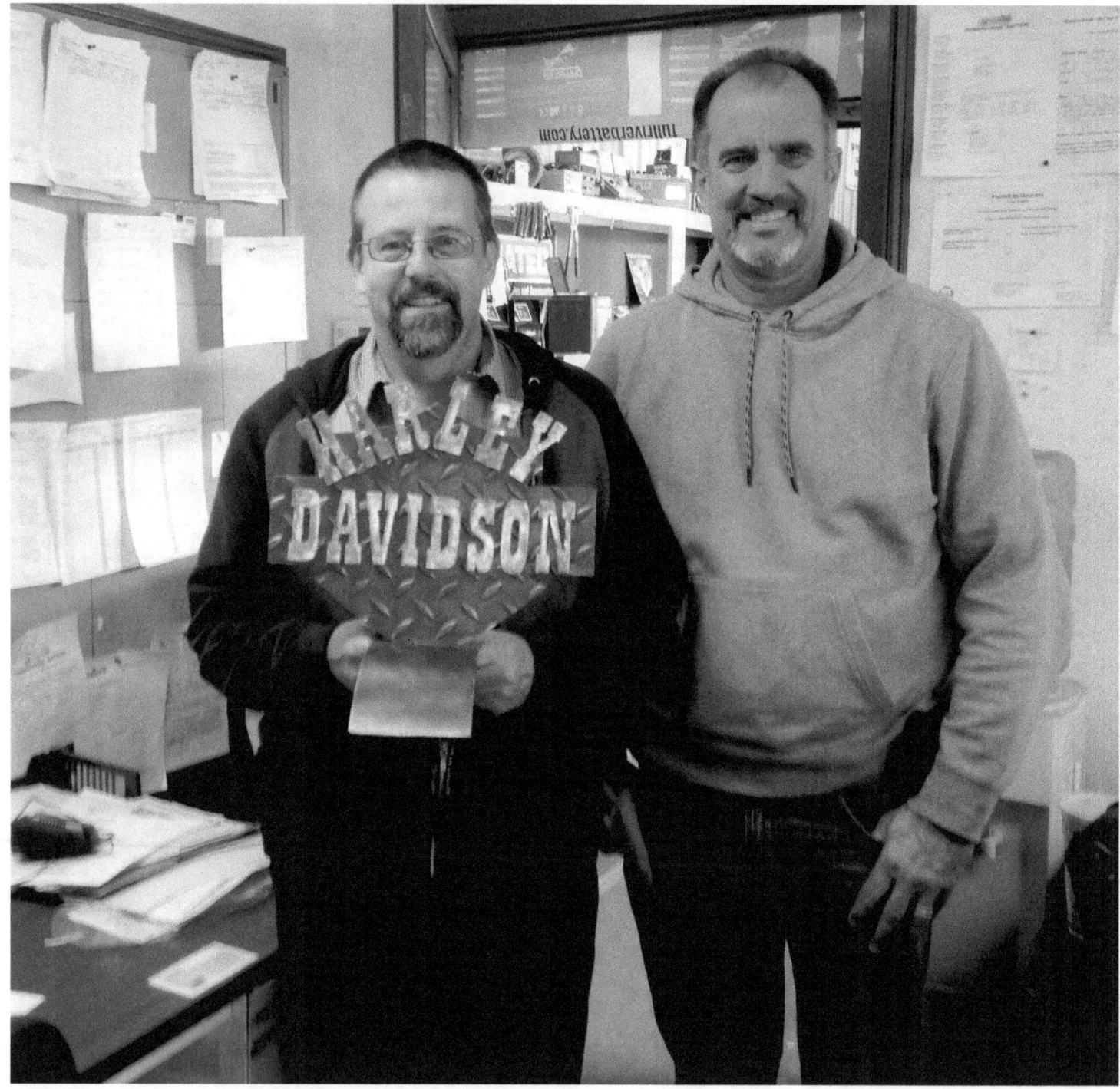

I work with Jeff and he kept telling me that he had a piece of metal shaped like the Harley logo that he wanted to see if I could work with. He finally brought it to me and I proceeded to mount it on a curved base that looked a bit like a cycle fender. Then I put the bronzed letters on it and gave it back to Jeff and his wife Tina who both ride Harleys.

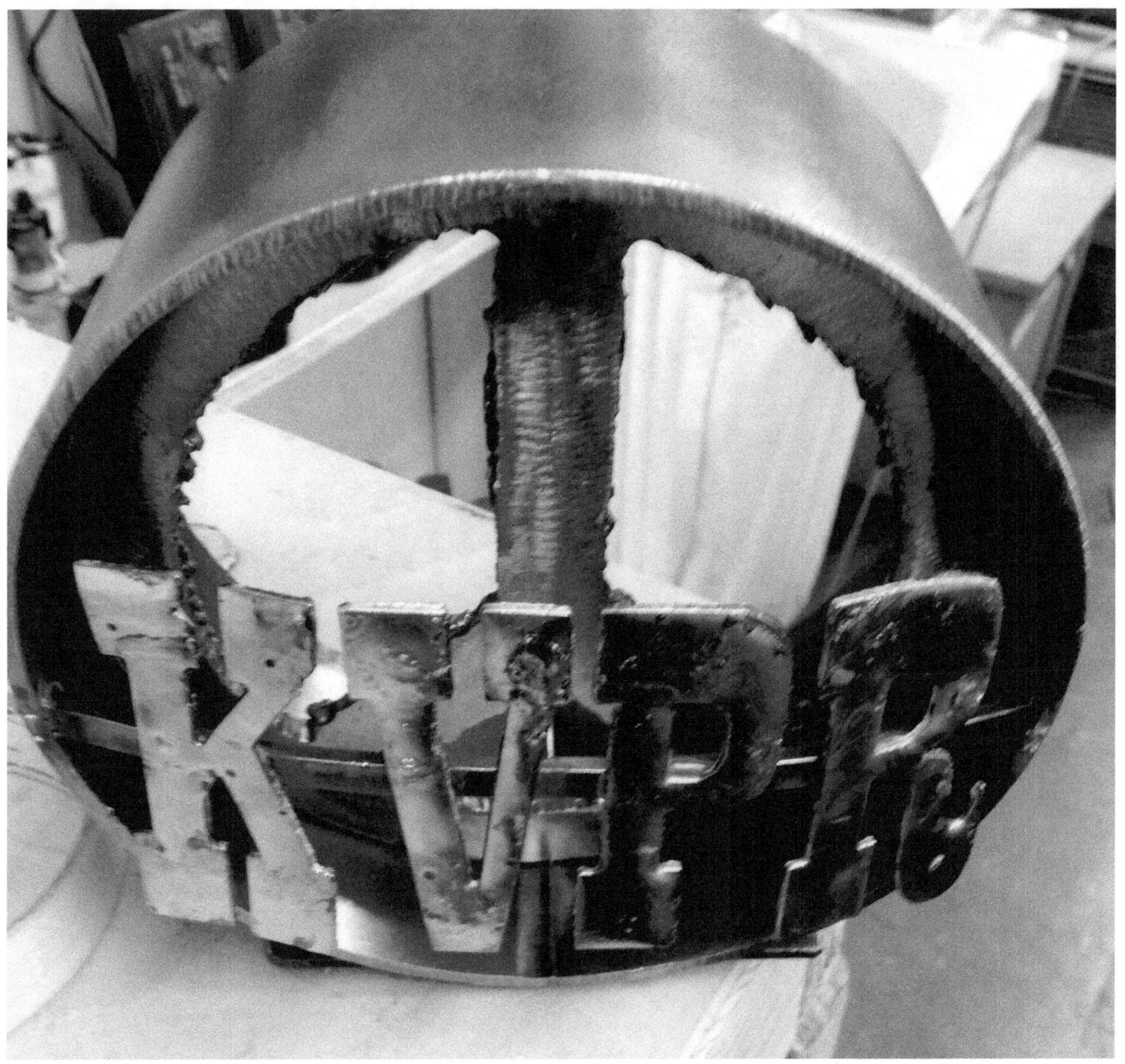

This was a piece I created for KVPR Radio in Fresno and Bakersfield as a thank you for using and promoting my two books on their public radio station. I really enjoy many of the programs on KVPR and find them very intellectually stimulating and a welcome departure to much of the mindless chatter that is found on other stations.

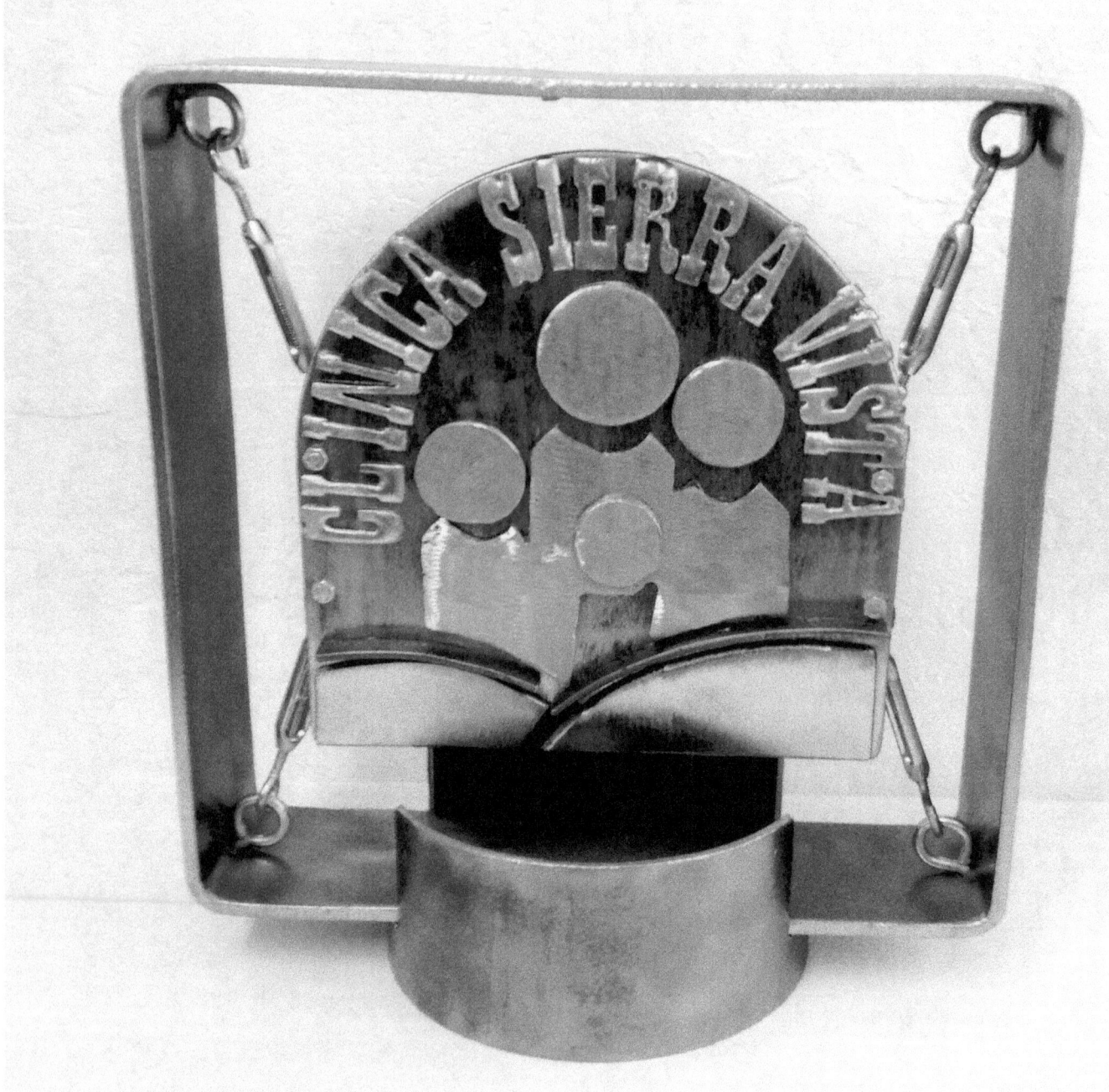

This was the first of three pieces commissioned by Clinica Sierra Vista Health Centers of California. I made this piece for their CEO, at the direction and suggestions of CSV. The center logo is hand cut out of plate steel and the steel letters are bronze coated. We also included two separate free standing metal plaques on which were some of the CEO's favorite quotes from Senator Edward Kennedy and JFK.

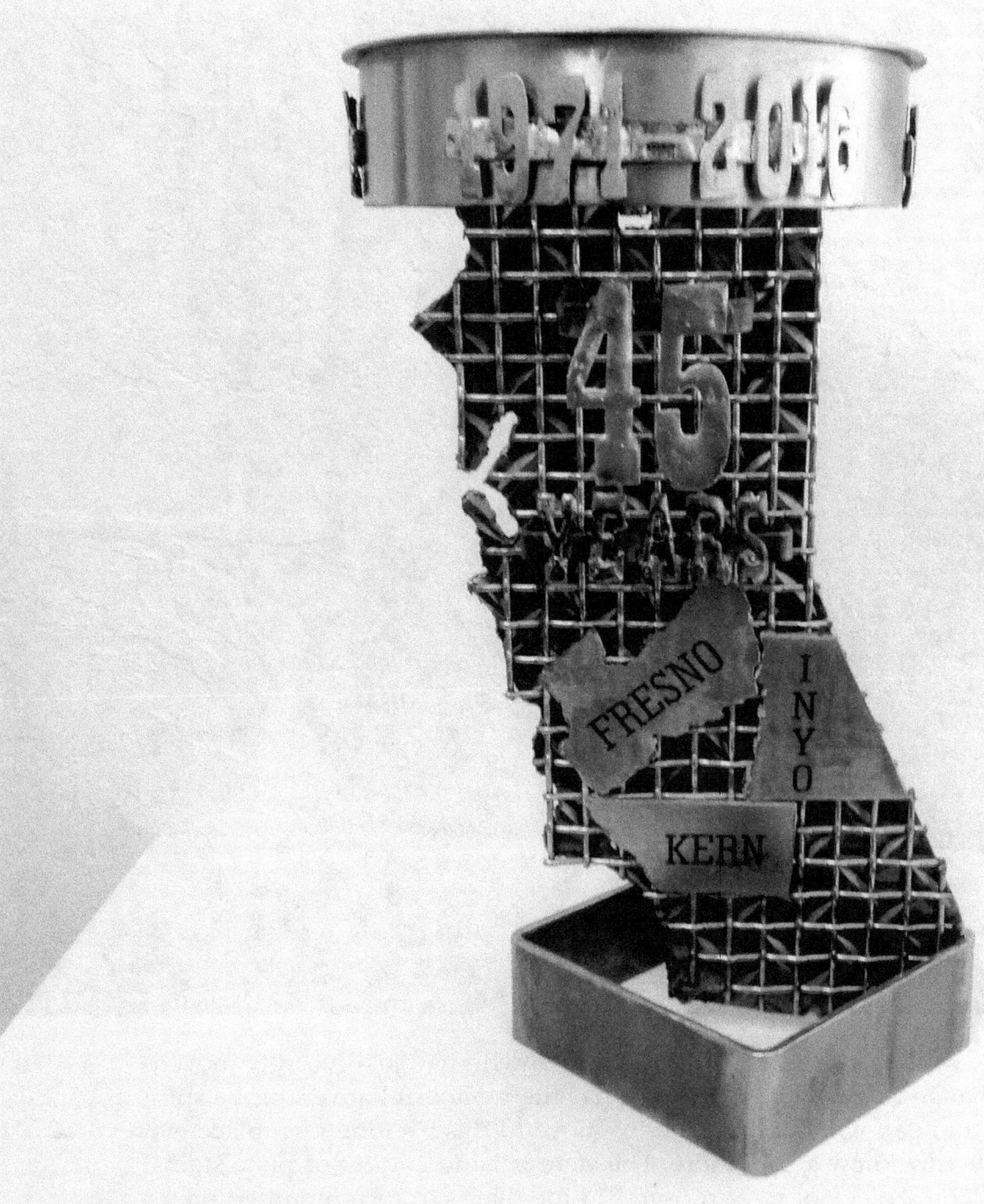

This is the second piece I built for Clinica Sierra Vista here in California. They are celebrating their forty fifth year in 2016. The first piece was a recognition for their CEO, the second is for their Kern office and the last piece will be for their Fresno office. I made each one distinctly different. This one is the state of California overlaid with a wire mesh. On it I cut out the three main counties where CSV operates. I mounted the round top on a bearing and it spins around displaying both the name and the years of operation...1971 to 2016.

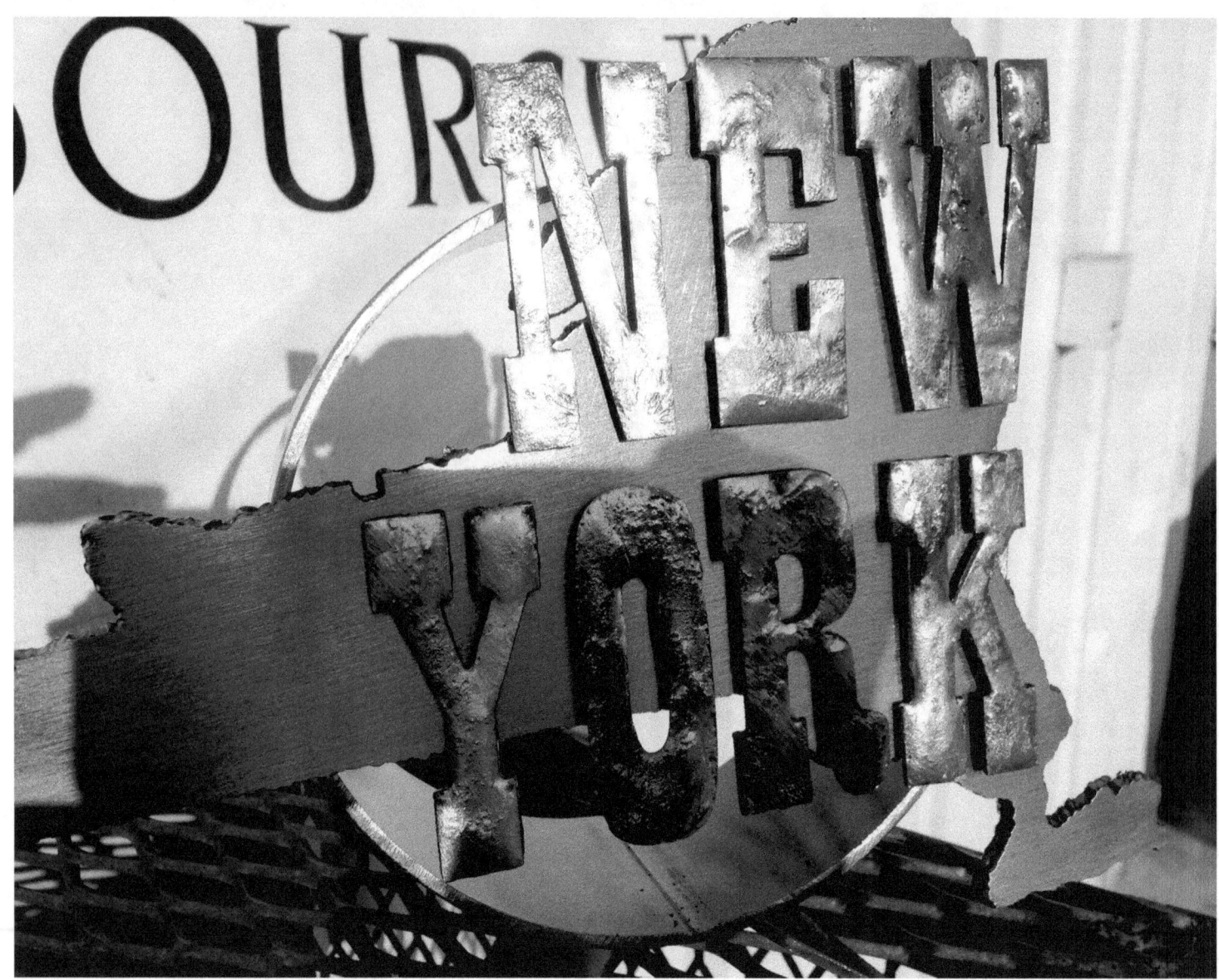

New York was for my wonderful niece Sarah who had just recently moved to Manhattan to take a new job. She has the wonderful adventurous spirit of her mom and dad which caused her to move to this exciting new place even though she hardly knew a soul there. The state is hand cut out of plate steel and mounted on a piece of re-purposed 8" pipe that is in turn mounted on a metal base. The letters are steel with bronze overlay welded on them and then polished with a hand grinder/buffer.

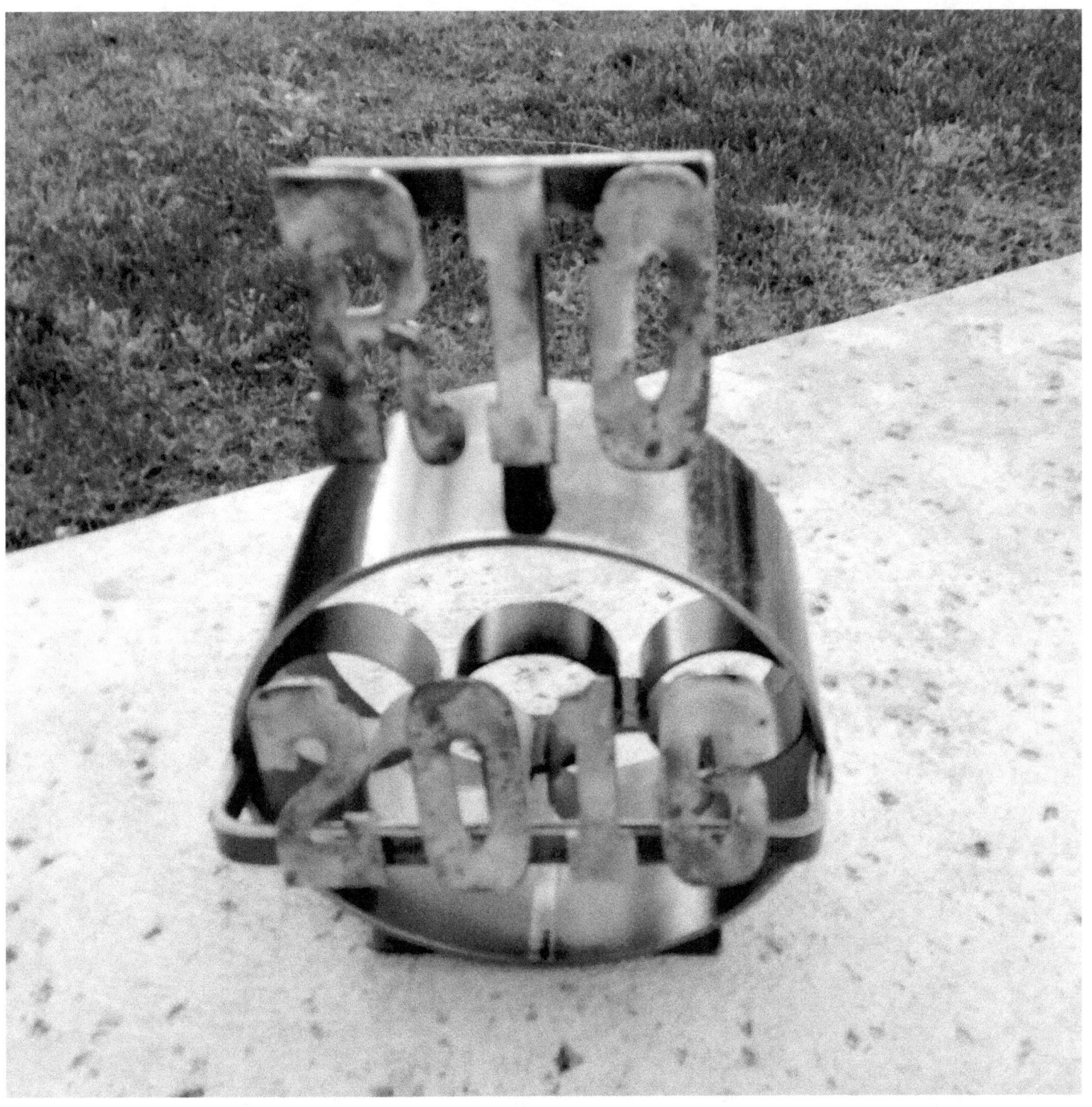

This was inspired from the upcoming 2016 Rio Olympics which we are all excited about. I think the main thing that fired me up about doing this piece was cutting the five rings out of an old piece of pipe that I had lying around. I then painted them in the appropriate Olympic colors. I donated it to our local public radio station for their silent auction fundraiser.

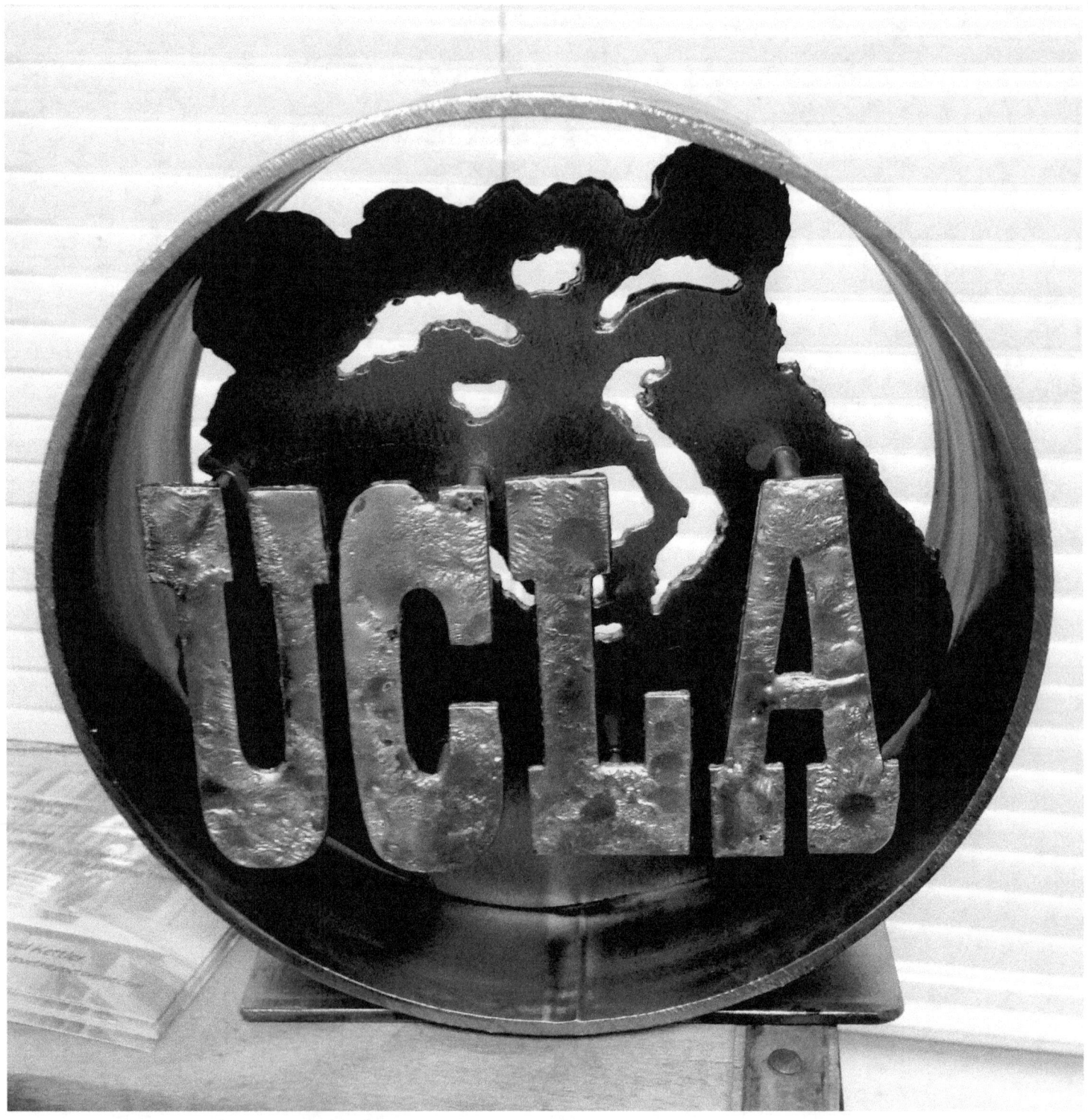

This piece was made for my oldest son, Douglas who graduated from UCLA. The bruin bear was a bit of a challenge because I cut him out with a hand torch rather than a plasma cutter. I thought it turned out well and we intend to get a picture of all three boys holding their respective art pieces when Doug visits.

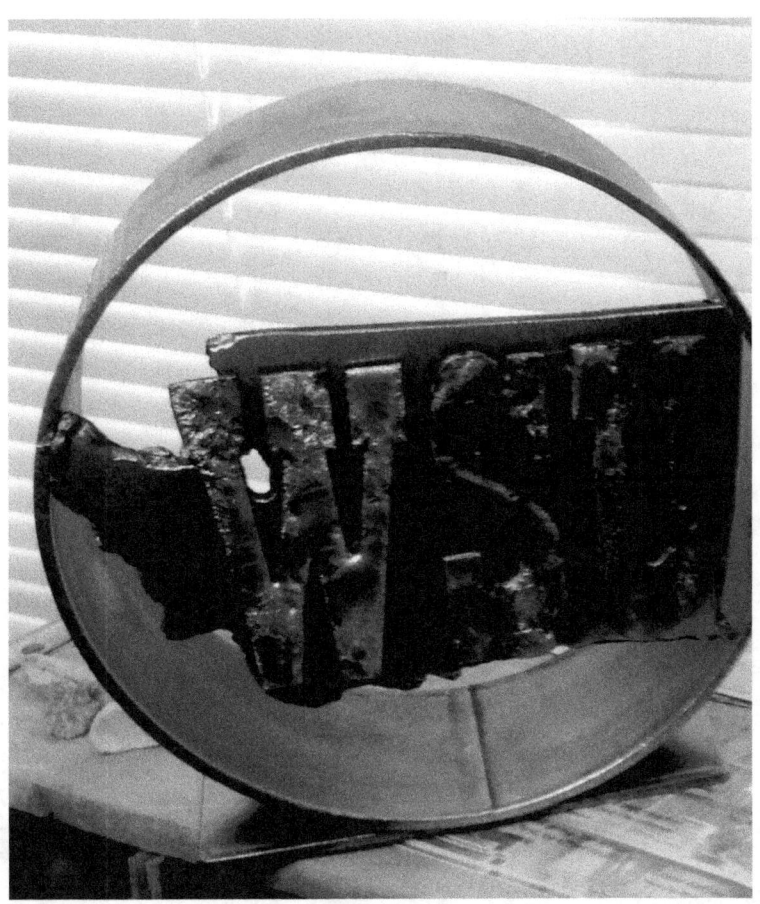

WSU was done for my good friend Eugene who used to live in Bakersfield and now lives in the Spokane area. He saw my metal pieces and had me make two WSU pieces for friends of his that were big fans, and also I did a larger Washington State piece for him that had a model of the Space Needle on it. These were cut out of 8" pipe with a metal cut-out of the state of Washington mounted inside. Attached are bronzed metal letters. Our friends Scott and Shelly are big fans of WSU as well even though their daughter now is a Husky on a full ride scholarship! Wonder how that's going to work out in the family!?

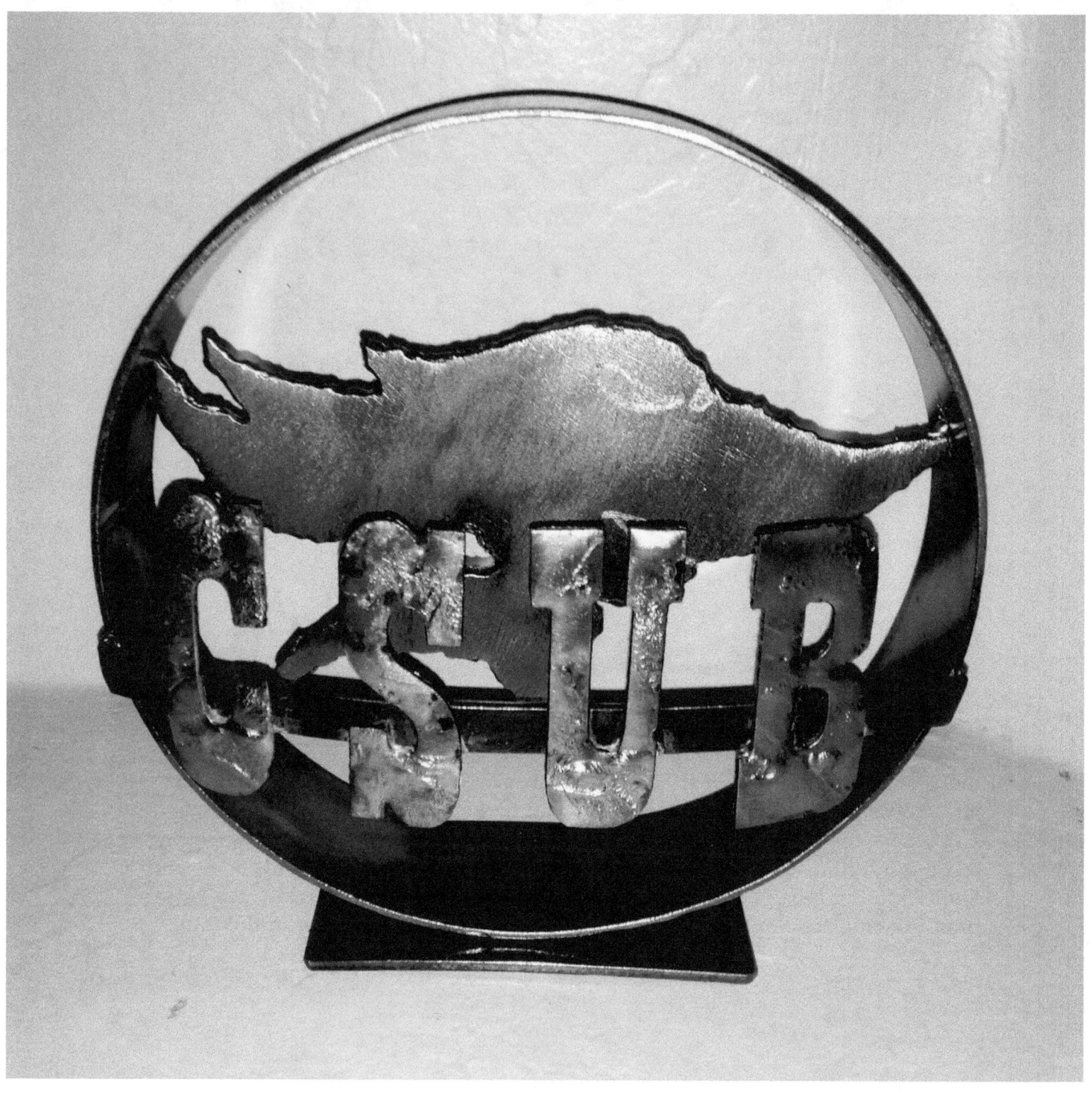

I did this piece for my son Brett when he graduated from Cal State Bakersfield. He had a great time at CSUB and enjoyed his years playing golf for them.

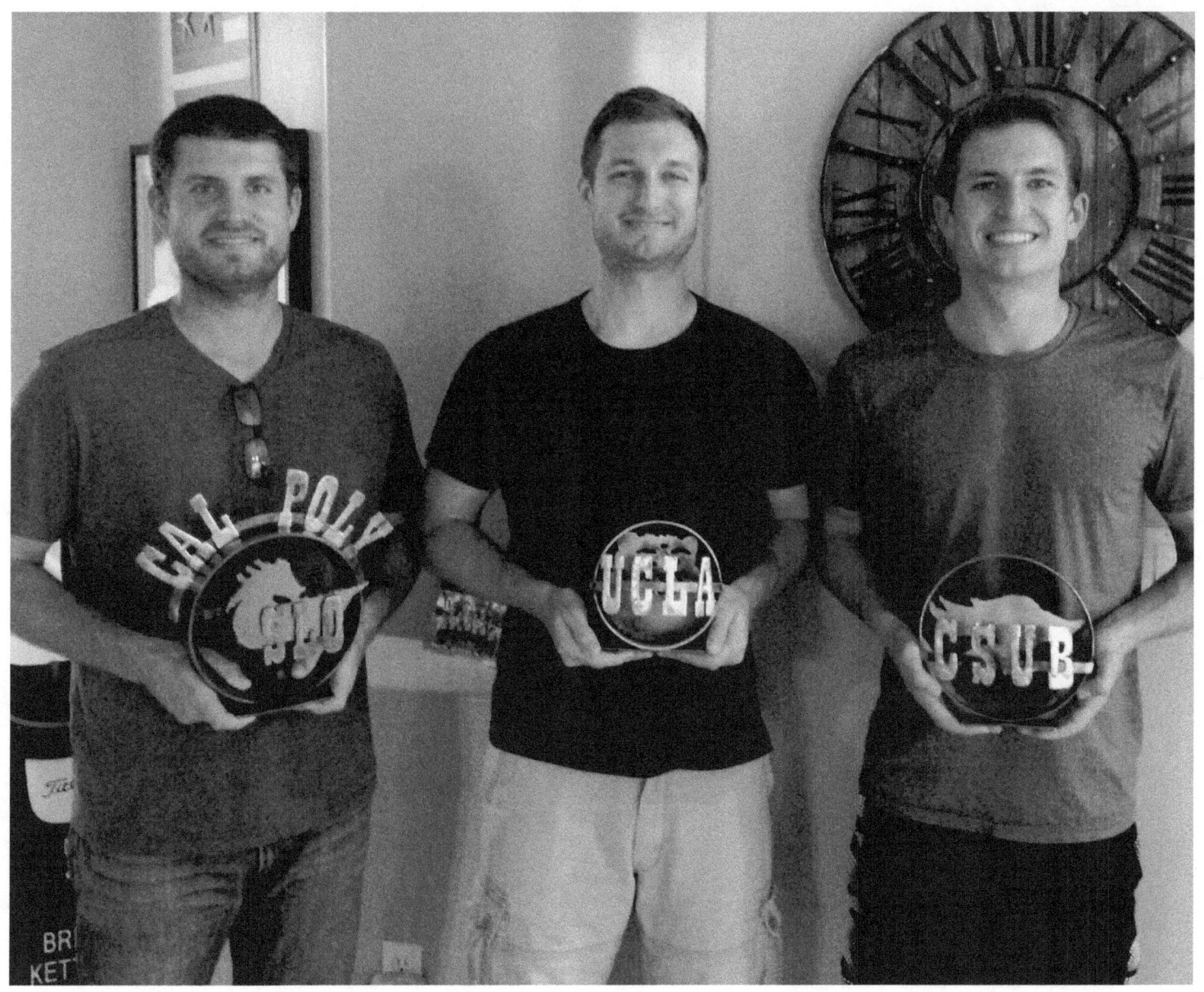

This is all three boys...Darren, Douglas and Brett holding their school art pieces. Doug was recently home from Jacksonville for Brett's graduation.

Art Display

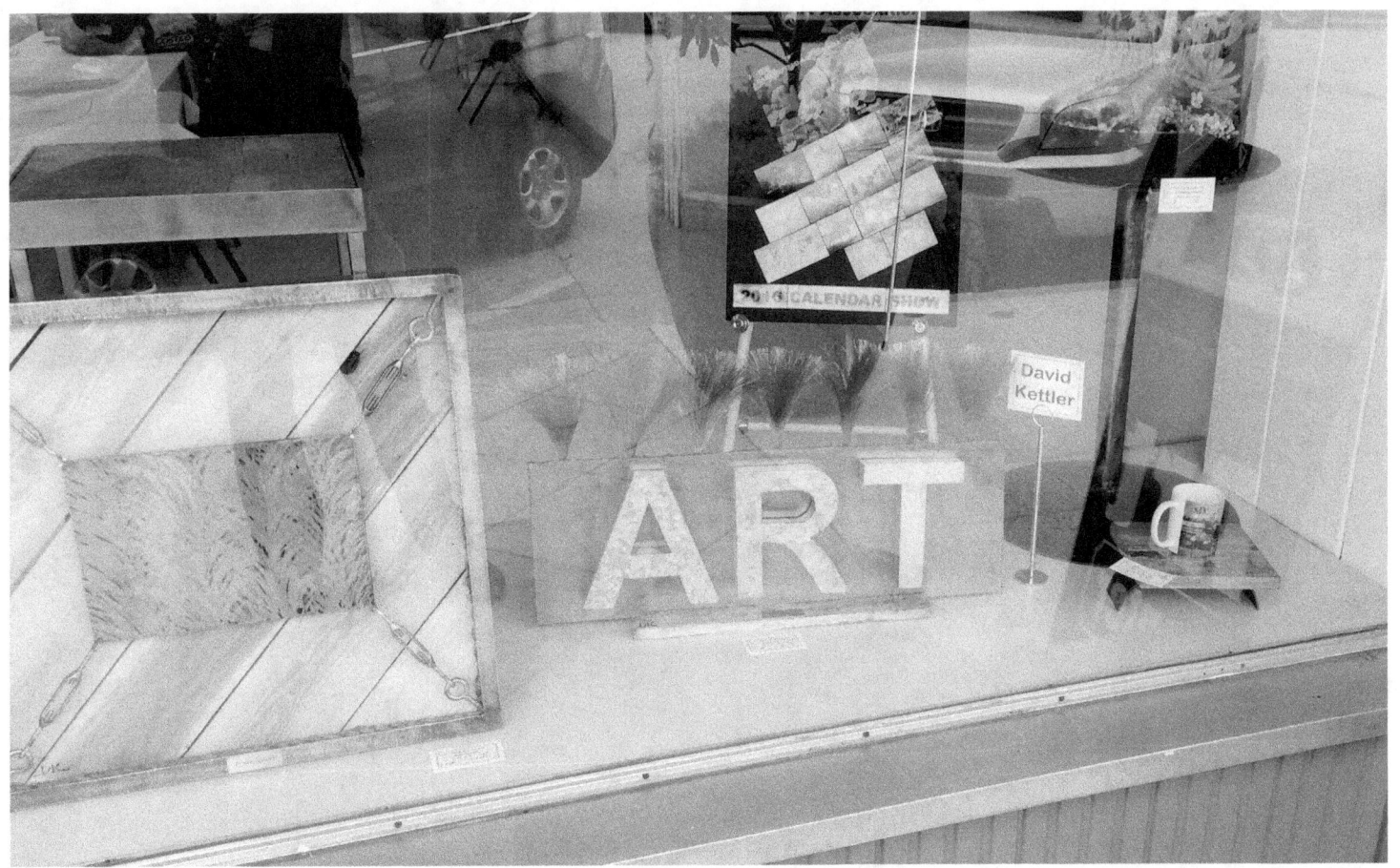

It was nearly a year ago that I met Iva, the President of Bakersfield Art Association. We attended some writing and poetry get-together's in the home of Jim and Kathleen's in Bakersfield. I had mentioned to Iva that I had made a wall mount piece of art using re-purposed metal and old shipping pallet wood and I wondered if they would like to hang it in their art gallery. She told me to create two more somewhat different pieces to show a broader style of my artwork, and then the board would analyze my work and vote on whether to accept it into the gallery or not. They liked my work. About two months later a window space opened up and my artwork has been displayed there ever since. Iva along with the association manager, Toni have been extremely supportive of my artwork and I have been most appreciative! I have come to know many of the artists that make up the BAA and I am very impressed by their acceptance, their kindness to me and the extreme talent represented in their many different styles and types of art.

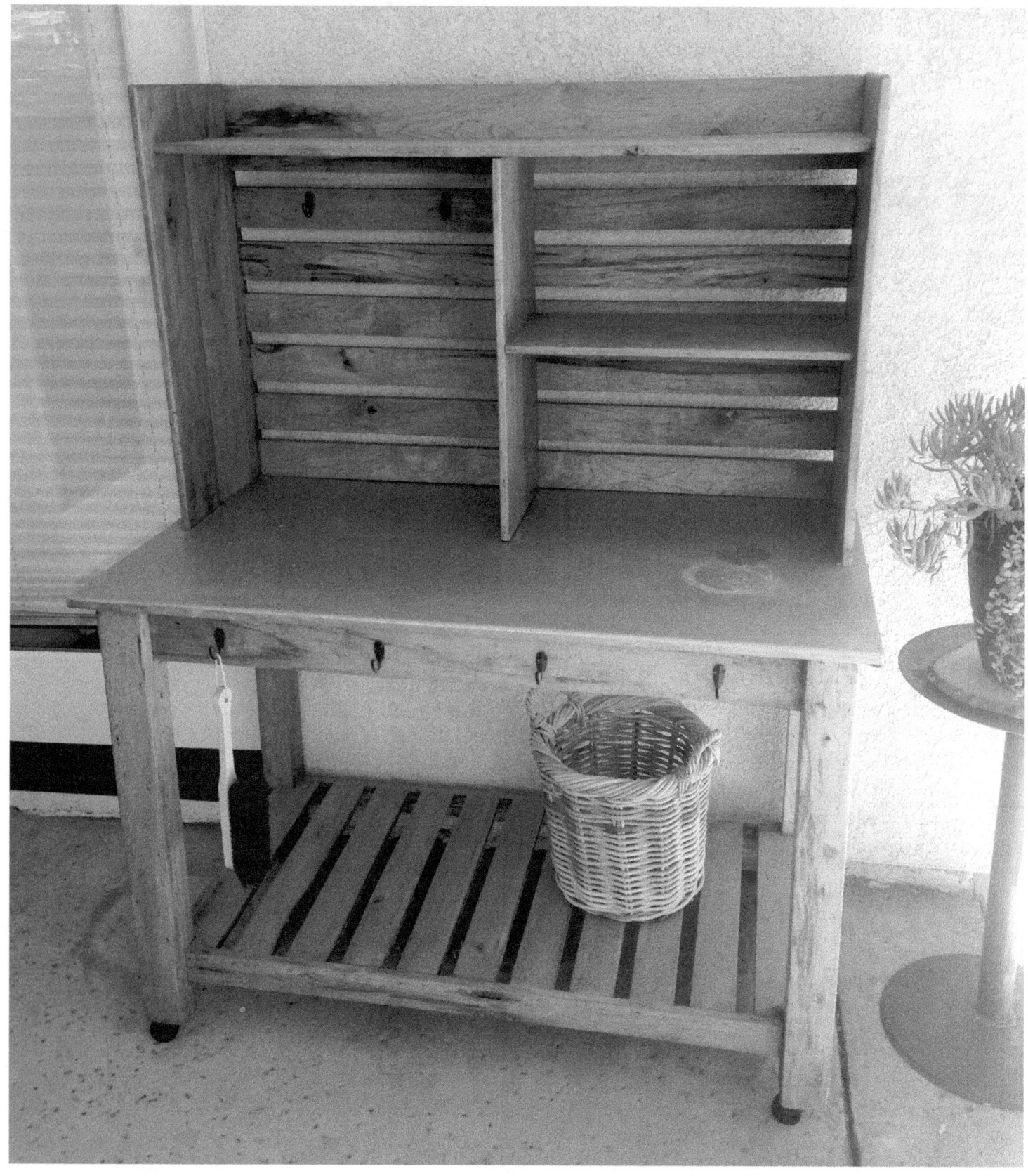

This piece was built by my very talented brother-in-law, Larry and it graces our back yard! The picture does not do it justice as it is a beautiful piece of furniture. Thanks Larry!

About the Artist

About the Artist

I'm so right brained that my left brained brother just thinks I'm "hare-brained!" I am a poet, an author and the creator of metal sculptures. My books are available on Amazon.com under my name. If it's a book about Karl Mannheim or social thought…that's not me, that's the other David Kettler!! "One Smart Antelope" is about living a balanced life in a very un-balanced world, and "My Reasons in Rhyme" is a collection of my poetry along with comments on why I wrote the poem, where I wrote it… etc.

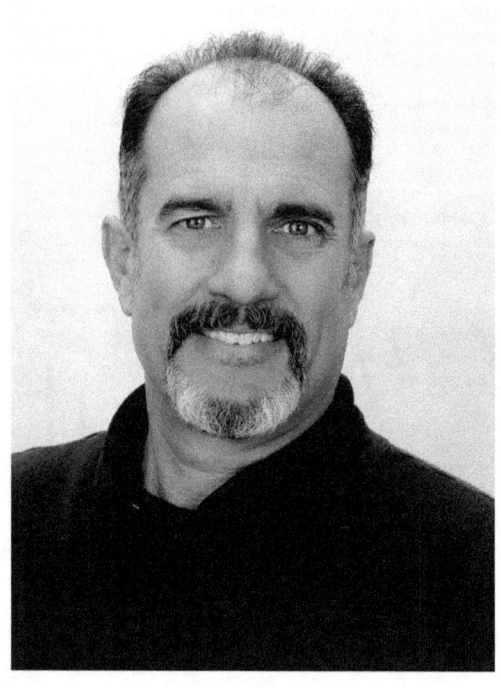

To try and track my creativity…I guess we could go back to childhood where it always seemed like I was trying to build a better bicycle out of some old junk! I remember welding "side-cars" onto our bicycles and it seemed that the welds would break at the most in-opportune time sending our passenger rolling along in the dirt! When I think that myself or none of my buddies came out of childhood with anything more than broken arms and bruises…I bow my head in thanks! Miracles do exist!

Another indicator of my sculpting ability would I guess appear in my twenties through my forties when if we were vacationing anywhere near the beach I would end up spending countless hours constructing huge sand sculptures consisting of whales, dolphins, manta rays, snakes and who knows what else! My long-suffering wife says that I have an inordinate need for attention…I guess all the people at the beach coming up and saying how cool it looked fueled that just a bit!? "How do you do that?" That is by far the question I most remember. My answer…" A lot of hard work and sunburn!" How I shaped the heads, tails, wings and snouts was just something that I saw in my mind and then tried my best to translate onto the sand as long as the sand would stay moist and not cave in! The other enemy was the tide! Just when the project was beginning to be ogled and awed…a rogue wave would make it look like an undecipherable mound of oatmeal!

A couple of years ago, I just started doing the same thing with metal and wood and I don't have to worry about the tide wrecking it! This hobby has been extremely gratifying and I hope you enjoy perusing the pictures.